INVENTING THE
FUTURE

Books by Marilee Zdenek

The Right-Brain Experience

Splinters in My Pride

Someone Special

*God Is a Verb**

*Catch the New Wind**

* *God Is a Verb* and *Catch the New Wind*
were written in collaboration
with Marge Champion.

INVENTING THE
FUTURE

———◆———

Advances in Imagery That
Can Change Your Life

MARILEE ZDENEK

McGraw-Hill Book Company

New York   St. Louis   San Francisco   Bogotá
Hamburg   Madrid   Mexico   Milan   Montreal
Panama   Paris   São Paulo   Tokyo   Toronto

First Paperback edition 1988

1 2 3 4 5 6 7 8 9 FGR FGR 8 9 0 9 8

ISBN 0-07-072819-4

LIBRARY OF CONGRESS CATALOGING-IN-PUBLICATION DATA

Zdenek, Marilee.
  Inventing the future.

  1. Success. 2. Intellect—Problems, exercises, etc.
3. Problem solving—Problems, exercises, etc. I. Title.
BF637.S8Z37 1987   158'.1   86-10330
ISBN 0-07-072819-4

Editing Supervisor: Margery Luhrs
Book Design by Kathryn Parise

For my mother,
Perla Dickason Earle,
who has always encouraged my dreams

CONTENTS

Contents

ACKNOWLEDGMENTS

On many Saturday and Sunday afternoons, four psychiatrists and a psychobiologist who are curious about the creative process and exceptionally generous of spirit, came to my home to test the exercises in this book. Mary Christianson, M.D., Helen Pankowsky, M.D., Barbara Sax, M.D., Bruce Christianson, M.D., and Jay Myers, Ph.D., became active participants in the program and allowed me to lead them through all the Inner Vision exercises. They experienced each Working Dream on a subjective basis and permitted me to report many of their experiences in the personal stories at the end of the chapters. This book, and all of us who invest ourselves in its message, are enriched by their insights and suggestions.

In addition, I am grateful for the responses of private clients, seminar participants, and colleagues who reported their experiences and who also agreed that I might share their personal responses to Inner Vision: Ron Field, choreographer; Gunnar Wessman, corporate executive; Leonora Langley, journalist; Bill Champlin, musician; and Dominic Molloy, computer systems analyst. Three of my own experiences are reported in these pages and are assigned to my alter ego, Kate. Those who allowed me to reveal particularly sensitive material and asked that their names be withheld know that their confidentiality will be maintained; I'm grateful for their trust.

Roger Sperry, Ph.D., who received the Nobel Prize in 1981 for his "split-brain" research and now devotes himself to exploring its implications for human values and consciousness, has given me the gift of his friendship and advice. A delightful and sometimes skeptical mentor, he has encouraged me to sustain the dream of peace and survival in a better world and to work for that reality.

Hans Weizel, M.D., is a professor of immunology at the Karolinska Institute in Stockholm, Sweden, and a member of the nominating committee for the Nobel Prize; we spent many hours discussing the immune system's response to mental imagery and his insights made a strong impact on my thinking.

Roger Fisher, professor at Harvard Law School and founder of The Harvard Negotiation Project, attended a workshop I presented when we were both speakers at EMF's (European Management Foundation's) Davos Symposium in Switzerland. I appreciate his challenging me to find a more appropriate word than "imagery" or "visualization" to describe a powerful experience that involves not only the eyes but all of the senses as well. *The Working Dream* came to mind as a more accurate term for the experience and I'm pleased that Professor Fisher functioned as such a delightfully effective catalyst.

I appreciate the contributions of psychologists Elizabeth Carlin, Ph.D., and Maury Carlin, Ph.D., who provided insights into the process of bonding and separation in the chapter on parent-child relationships. My thanks also go to entertainer Stevie Wonder and novelist Harriet Doerr, who enhanced the chapter on compelling careers. Gerald Jampolsky, M.D., psychiatrist; Klaus D. Hoppe, M.D., Ph.D., psychoanalyst; and writer Leo Buscaglia each made specific contributions to this material. Stanley J. Leiken, M.D., psychoanalyst, has influenced my thinking on many of the subjects addressed in these pages and I'm grateful for his interest and encouragement.

Imagery for the Working Dream was inspired by Jungian symbolism, surrealist paintings, science fiction films, and children's literature; especially valuable were *The Little Prince, The Velveteen Rabbit, Alice in Wonderland, The Wizard of Oz, Remember the Night Rainbow,* and *Peter Pan.*

I'm pleased to be working once again with my editor, Lou Ashworth, whose suggestions and support are greatly appreciated. My literary agent, Don Congdon, provided excellent advice, as always, and his commitment to this book has been affirming. Amy

Louise Shapiro was my first reader and offered comments on the manuscript that were extremely helpful. My husband, Albert N. Zdenek, M.D., provided an abundance of encouragement and welcomed celebrations along the way—I'm grateful for his nurturing spirit. I have been influenced by my daughters, Gina and Tamara, who can always see the night rainbow when the sky is black, and whose perceptions I value. Administrative assistance has come from Gina Somers, who, with charm and efficiency, kept Right-Brain Resources, Inc. running smoothly during the time I was writing this book.

CHAPTER 1

INVENTING THE FUTURE

———◆———

The moment you alter your perception of yourself and your future, both you and your future begin to change.

There's a Native American fable about a young brave who took an egg from an eagle's nest and put it in a chicken yard. The egg hatched and the eagle grew up among the chickens, pecking in the ground for food as they did, scratching in the dust as he watched the others do. One day he looked up and saw an eagle soaring above him. He felt his wings trembling and he said to one of the chickens, "I wish I could do that."

"Don't be a fool," the chicken said, "only an eagle can fly so high."

Feeling ashamed of his longing, the eagle went back to scratching in the dirt—never again to question what he believed to be his assigned place on earth.

Let's rewrite the ending. Suppose the eagle had refused to allow someone else to define his potential. Suppose he had sensed his uniqueness and broken free, opened those powerful wings, and taken off over the heads of all the chickens who failed to recognize his true power and identity. Imagine how he would feel, stretching out for the first time to claim his destiny.

It's all a matter of perception. Before the eagle could fly, he had to alter his perception of himself and recognize that he did not belong in the situation where circumstances had placed him. Only then was he ready to move on.

But now let's create a variation on the tale: Once there was an Indian brave who took an egg from a chicken coop and placed it in an eagle's nest in a pine tree, on top of a high mountain. The chicken broke out of its shell, saw an eagle flying nearby and, wise chicken that he was, made a sound appraisal of his limitations. Fortunately for him, his instincts told him that it would take more than wishful thinking to achieve the skills to fly with those birds, no matter what twist of fate had placed him among them.

Always, there is the need for balance: the accurate assessment of potential and the realistic assessment of limitations. Who could deny the importance of both?

Between limitation and potential lies a vast area that is not predetermined by destiny but which is defined only by the individual choices of the one person at the heart of the story.

AGAINST THE ODDS

I think of Jeff Keith, who lost a leg to cancer when he was a child, but who, in 1985, when he was twenty-two years old, spent eight months running over three thousand miles across the United States. "I wanted to show that people like me are physically challenged, not physically handicapped," he said, as he turned over $120,000 in contributions to the American Cancer Society from people who had sponsored his historic run.

Jeff Keith refused to let the doubters hold him back. He wore out thirty-six pairs of sneakers and his artificial leg was replaced five times as he made his way across the country. In spite of the six-pound plastic leg with the hydraulic knee mechanism and an artificial foot with movable toes, he kept a pace of twelve miles a day. Obviously, Jeff's perception of himself and his situation was as important to his success as his physical strength.

PUTTING THE ODDS IN
YOUR FAVOR

Is there something in your life you would like to change? If so, first change your perception of the problem. When you can see yourself and your situation differently, you have already taken on the responsibility for your success.

You can learn to alter your point of view with very little effort and a great deal of pleasure. In fact, by the time you've read this book and played the games of imagination in each chapter, you should see significant improvement in your ability to take charge of important areas of your life. The process that enables you to have that power is called *Inner Vision*.

Inner Vision takes you through a sensual mental adventure that can influence your attitudes and convictions in a positive, productive way. This experience can lead to dramatic changes in the way you think about success and the actions you take to achieve it.

EXPERIENCING THE BEST OF BOTH SIDES
OF YOUR BRAIN

Scientific research has shown that both hemispheres of the brain work together for almost every activity, but that one hemisphere or the other will dominate for a specific type of task. Most brain researchers believe that the left side of the brain dominates for logical, analytical reasoning and for language skills; it processes information in a linear (one-step-at-a-time) sort of way. The right side of the brain dominates for spatial, imaginative, and artistic skills and it processes information in a nonlinear way, springing from one idea to another, experiencing sudden leaps of insight. On the right side of the brain, dreams and emotions are realized.

Inner Vision encourages the greatest use of your mental resources in both hemispheres of your brain. In three progressive steps you will experience:

- *The Transition*

- *The Working Dream*

- *The Dreamer and the Critic*

The Transition enables both hemispheres of the brain to become deeply relaxed; the right hemisphere may then gain dominance as it begins to play with the images that are suggested.

The Working Dream stimulates your visual, imaginative, intuitive powers—which involve the predominant use of the right hemisphere of your brain.

The Dreamer and the Critic draws upon the logical, analytical expertise of the brain's left hemisphere. In this third step in the Inner Vision process, you benefit from the combined insights of both sides of the brain.

Through this three-step process, which is described in detail in Chapter 2, you can alter your perception of yourself, your situation, and your future. When you have done that, change is already in progress.

These techniques are a means of transport into the secret parts of your being. They provide the diving bell that takes you into the depths of any experience—past or future—where, through memory and fantasy, you can explore options and unconscious needs. Inner Vision exercises become the rocket ship that carries you high above the realities of your problems to gain perspective and discover new insights. They are the mind-expanding vehicle that takes you from where you are now into the possibilities of the future.

A DIFFERENT WAY OF THINKING

In the last few years, I've worked with thousands of people in seminar situations, and I have discovered that there is a need for right-brain exercises that are directly applicable to specific problems. As president of Right-Brain Resources, Inc., I've had the opportunity to work with clients with diverse interests and backgrounds. Some use my program to live more creative and interesting lives; others apply these exercises to their professional activities.

A few months ago in London I met with a new client to discuss leading a seminar for his corporation. After a few hours, he asked me a direct and curious question: "After so many years of working with these techniques, do you still use them yourself?"

His question caused me to wonder how anyone could *not* want to use a process that makes the problems of life more easily surmountable? I use the exercises daily, in one form or another. Sometimes I use them to gain clarity on difficult problems; often I use them for relaxation, without conscious thought, as if I were simply breathing in and breathing out the process. Always, I use them with a sense of appreciation for how much more smoothly life works for me because of this program.

Although the Inner Vision process certainly hasn't turned me into Superwoman, it *has* released inner potential that was unavailable to me before I developed this program. It has made an extraordinary difference in the way I feel about myself and my work.

About fifteen years ago, I was invited to a university on the East Coast where a few guests were asked to speak on various aspects of the creative process. Before leaving Los Angeles I had felt excited and confident, pleased to be asked to participate in a symposium with a highly distinguished group of experts. After I arrived, my confidence began to diminish rapidly. As I listened to the other speakers—university professors, Renaissance scholars, the president of a prestigious seminary—I became painfully aware that I was standing there academically naked, without a single higher degree to cover my insecurities.

The others read their impressive and finely-honed lectures; I had planned to speak somewhat extemporaneously, using only a few notes. Suddenly I had no confidence in my straightforward, casual presentation. The distance between the other speakers and myself seemed to stretch into light-years and, in a desperate attempt to regain my self-esteem, I set out to try to minimize the gap.

I was the last speaker in that three-day conference, and when it was time for my part in the program, I had completely revised my presentation. I, too, spoke from a prepared text; spontaneous phrases were replaced by carefully worded thoughts. Where a simple word would have been fine, I found a more pretentious one. It was, as you can well imagine, quite dreadful. Never have I given such a dreary speech . . . and never have I learned so much from my mistakes.

I resolved then that I would never pretend to be other than who I am, not by words and not by attitudes. And I decided that the real problem in that situation was my *perception* of the other people and of my relationship to them.

Recently I encountered a situation that strangely echoed that experience from years ago. And yet my reaction—and the results—were dramatically different. In Davos, Switzerland, there is a most extraordinary symposium held each year to provide both political and economic world leaders with a forum for "an informal exchange of ideas." In 1985, Raymond Barre, former Prime Minister of France, was chairman of the event, which is known as EMF's (European Management Foundation's) Davos Symposium. Speakers were heads of state (past or present) from England, Germany, Switzerland, and Turkey. Ambassadors were there in profusion, including Jeane Kirkpatrick, who had just resigned her position as Ambassador to the United Nations. Participants came to the symposium from over fifty countries, from New Zealand, China, the Middle East, South America, the United States, and Western Europe. Also attending the symposium were corporate presidents and executive officers from many of the Fortune 500 companies.

Because people in positions of leadership are aware of the need to think creatively, to develop intuition and to see problems from various perspectives, I was invited to present two briefings addressing those issues. Each session was an hour and a half in length and included a speech and some of the mental exercises I use in my seminars.

Any truthful person who tells you he's never experienced the anxiety of confronting his own vulnerability is either out of touch with his feelings or hasn't taken on many challenges. I am attracted to challenges as the snow leopard is attracted to mountain tops, but I sometimes feel as vulnerable as a child trying to learn to run.

When the invitation came for me to speak at the Davos Symposium, I experienced more than a moment of wondering whether the techniques that have worked so effectively in the United States and for a few European clients would appeal to such a culturally diverse audience. And considering the various other seminars scheduled at the same time, discussing matters of global importance, I wondered if the participants would want to attend a seminar entitled *The Right-Brain Experience: An Intimate Program to Free the Powers of Your Imagination.*

I'm certainly not an expert on politics or economics, but I do know some things about enhancing mental capacity. And I know how to help people get in touch with their deepest feelings and gain clarity about what they need and what they want. World leaders, whether in political, economic, or other realms, have often paid a high price for their success, and I believe that these techniques can help them deal with their anxieties.

The difference between my perception of that university setting fifteen years ago and the present situation was simply this: Long ago, I thought of myself as a woman whose gifts were minimal compared with those of the other speakers; at the Davos Symposium, I perceived my gifts as *different* from theirs and focused on the value of my own program. This allowed me to thoroughly enjoy their excellent lectures and stimulating briefings without feeling competitive with them. To ensure that I would be at my best when it was my turn to speak (and without considering our respective places in the world's pecking order), I prepared my mind by following the same type of exercises that I teach others to use.

Long before I arrived in Switzerland, I had mentally envisioned what I wished would happen. What is essential is the fact that by intentionally determining my perspective, I created the *climate* that was conductive to success.

In an Inner Vision exercise, I had imagined that I would feel relaxed and confident and that the audience would be receptive. At the symposium itself, I did feel at ease with my audience and they were as warm and enthusiastic as I had hoped. In my mind's eye, I had envisioned that not everyone in the room would agree with my ideas, and that I would not feel threatened if some of their questions reflected negative attitudes. But in reality, almost everyone was willing to close his eyes and experience the exercises, and only one of the many questions following the lecture seemed critical. In my fantasy, I had imagined that the exercises would cut across cultural barriers and that some of the people there would want to work with me in a more extensive program; before I left Switzerland, seminar inquiries had come from people from France, England, Belgium, Turkey, Switzerland, and New Zealand.

The fifteen years that passed between those two events have brought considerable changes in my life. Surely there has been growth through education and personal experience that would account for some of the differences in my response. But I know that what made the biggest difference was the use of the mental techniques that allowed me to perceive myself and my situation in the most constructive way.

DEFINING WHAT YOU WANT

Not everyone would enjoy leading seminars and what seems like success to me might be regarded quite differently by someone else. Success is a relative word, defined in a myriad of ways, and we must each find our own understanding of what that term means in our lives.

Some people want to be at the top of the financial ladder; others want to check out of the system and simplify living. For still others, "winning" means gaining control of their lives in extremely personal ways—such as learning to avoid destructive thought patterns, discovering how to be more sensitive to the feelings of others, getting in touch with their own deepest longings.

Inner Vision is far more than a motivational tool. It is an experiential process that enables you to *know who you are, know what you need,* and *see the possibilities for change.* Whether your goal is to excel in your work, to be successful in personal relationships, or to have greater control over your attitudes and actions, the process of Inner Vision is a fascinating adjunct to more traditional tools for success.

Henry David Thoreau recognized the use of imagination for reaching one's goals. He wrote in *Walden,* "If one advances confidently in the direction of his dreams, and endeavors to live the life which he has imagined, he will meet with a success unexpected in common hours."

In Gary Zukav's delightful book on the subject of the new physics, *The Dancing Wu Li Masters,* he expressed this enchanting thought:

> Reality is what we take to be true. What we take to be true is what we believe. What we believe is based upon our perceptions. What we perceive depends upon what we look for. What we look for depends upon what we think. What we think depends upon what we perceive. What we perceive determines what we believe. What we believe determines what we take to be true. What we take to be true is our reality.

Take care what you believe to be true, for through your beliefs your reality is formed.

CHAPTER 2

STARTING FROM
WHERE YOU ARE

———◆———

"Dreams are real while they last; can we say more of life?" wrote Havelock Ellis. Dreams have a certain reality all their own; in the unconscious mind, they play out the dark side of the wishes and fears we experience in conscious awareness. Dreams send us messages from the deepest parts of ourselves; they often give us pleasure and they occasionally warn us of dangers that we perceive at the unconscious level; they hint of solutions to situations that trouble us in our usual waking state.

Dreams come to us when we sleep and they come to us when we make the transition from normal consciousness to a deep state of reverie. In either situation, it is possible for a dream to become so vivid that we feel as though we are transported to another place and time. Dreams that occur during sleep are difficult for most people to remember, but in reverie we are fully aware of what is happening to us in the dream. We have the ability to control our responses and actions and we can choose to learn from the insights that are revealed in the experience. When we discover how to do this, the common daydream is intensified and transformed from ordinary fantasy to a practical and evocative tool for exploring the inner landscape; it is referred to in this book as the Working Dream.

After a few sessions of Inner Vision exercises, many people report that their Working Dream imagery is highly fanciful and rich in metaphors; others experience the Dream as intense in feeling but the imagery is tied more closely to reality. It is important to remember that whether your images are practical or exotic, they nonetheless reveal valuable messages from the unconscious.

KATE'S WORKING DREAM

I am free . . . light . . . floating. I soar without effort above the green jungle. The air is warm . . . I feel the clouds touch my cheeks . . . I fly through the rainbow and wrap the colors around me, swirling them over my head, letting them flow from my hand like a long scarf. When I drop the rainbow it forms again in an arch across the sky. I float on nothingness, slowly descending through an opening in the trees, landing softly on the jungle floor.

Two majestic creatures, powerful and elegant are waiting there for me. I don't speak to the tiger, though he seems gentle and soft. It is the panther that draws me toward him in the lush ferns. And the panther seems to say to me, 'I'm glad you're not afraid; if you had been afraid, I would have growled.' I say, 'But I am afraid; isn't it all right to tell you how I feel?' And although the panther does not speak, I know that it is not all right to show my feelings.

Suddenly, and without any discomfort at all, I am absorbed by the panther and it feels fine to be part of this sleek and powerful creature. We move through the jungle and I feel the excitement of being part of his power and elegance. . . . It feels as if I have *become* the panther . . . but now the feeling is changing and I don't want to be here. I don't want to be alive in the panther's body. My identity is diminished. . . . I tell the panther how I feel and he says to me, 'Well, go home then.' And I do. Flying up through the clearing in the trees, I am aware that the tiger is watching me and smiling. I bring myself back to this room with the strong realization that something important has happened in the dream.

To experience such a wild dream even in sleep would surely seem bizarre, even to the most fanciful dreamers. Many people would choose to just roll over and forget it—but then they wouldn't benefit from the meaning that is hidden in the metaphor of the tiger and the panther and the jungle flight.

Kate experienced this dream while she was with a group of twenty-five writers who were learning how to use mental imagery and other right-brain techniques to stimulate creative thinking. Because she was awake during the dream (though in a deeply relaxed state) it was easy for her to remember all that happened in it. Kate recorded the experience in her Working Dream notebook using the present tense (which is always the most effective way to recall any kind of dream) and then read it to the group.

Then the critical work began. Kate began interpreting her dream by making note of the characters, events, and feelings in her story. Instead of using a linear process in reporting what she had imagined, she made notes at random, in whatever order they came to mind, circling each one.

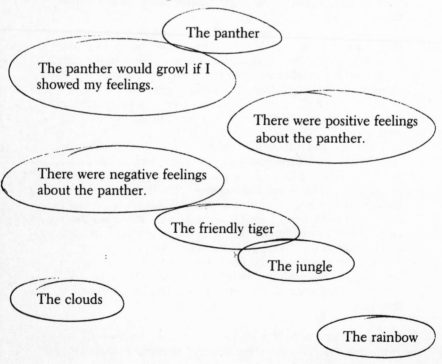

Kate thought that her playfulness with the clouds and the rainbow represented her need for personal and artistic expression; flying made her feel a sense of power and freedom. The panther reminded her of the publisher who had just made an offer on her book; it was an impressive corporation, powerful in the literary community. The fact that the panther would growl if she expressed her feelings reminded her of the phone conversation with the editor at the publishing house. He had not seemed at all pleased when Kate objected to some changes he wanted, which she felt would have been pretentious and not in harmony with her own style.

In the Dream, she had felt good about being part of the sleek and elegant panther, just as she had enjoyed fantasizing about being published by such a prestigious company. But then Kate had felt anxious about being absorbed by the panther, and she resented the loss of personal identity. What does a writer have, if not her individuality of thought? And what is the point of working with such an important publisher, if you feel devoured by their demands?

It wasn't clear who the tiger represented. However, only three days later, Kate received a second offer for her book from an equally substantial publisher who didn't want her to change anything at all. "I suppose my tiger was an unconscious symbol of confidence," she said. "I trusted my work and knew that someone would emerge from the wilds of the literary world who would let me express what I feel in my own way."

The Working Dream, which allowed Kate's anxieties to be focused in elucidating imagery, helped her to define her deepest feelings and clarify her decision.

Dreams are clearly biased toward emotional needs, and that is an important fact to keep in mind. When you have learned to read the messages from your unconscious, you will still need to draw on the wise critic of your analytical self. This will provide you with balance between the emotional and the intellectual evaluations.

You may wonder how Kate was able to let her imagination play with such exotic images in a waking state. You may also wonder if she is a tad peculiar, wandering around in daydreams in the belly of a panther, playing with rainbows, and flying over the jungle. But if you've learned to invoke the powers of your own personal imagery, you know just how valuable such fantasies can be. Not everyone has Working Dreams as fanciful as Kate's. If you are just beginning to play with the Working Dream, you may be content to experience less exotic imagery—at least until you've learned to trust the process.

Before Kate took off for her flight over the jungle, she had experienced a mental exercise for making the transition from normal consciousness to a deep, dreamlike state that is similar to an exercise that will appear later in this chapter. After she was deeply relaxed, it was suggested that she would cross over a bridge into a land where she would have great power. Then she was told that she would meet someone who would help her clarify her feelings about a very important situation in her life. Although she was led into the experience by these suggestions, it was Kate who created the specific metaphors within the Working Dream.

The twenty-five people in that workshop all heard the same suggestions, but they had twenty-five totally different experiences within the Dream. No one else in that room talked to animals that day. One man chose to return to his childhood home and dreamed of a conversation with his grandfather, who had always seemed like a wise and caring mentor in his younger life. Another man chose to dream of England, where he hoped to go to finish his novel. He could imagine the house he would live in and see it in his mind's eye. He imagined meeting a woman on the country road who gave him insights into one of the characters in his story. Somehow the Dream made his goal seem more possible and later, in his evaluation of the Dream, he began to seriously consider spending time in a small village near the border of England and Wales.

In the Working Dream, you will encounter suggestions that provide a structure for the freedom of your imagination; this structure allows you to express your own imagery within the framework of the suggestions.

Before we consider the various uses for the Working Dream, or the need for your good inner Critic to give balance to your visions, we need to consider the first step in the program: the Transition.

HOW THE TRANSITION WORKS

The relaxation exercise provided in this first step of the program is designed to produce alpha waves in both hemispheres of the brain. Alpha waves alter the normal state of consciousness, enabling you to enter a dreamlike state of awareness while remaining awake. This first part of the Transition exercise includes adaptations of some classic techniques for relaxation. Variations of this exercise have been tested in medical research programs, stress reduction centers, and by most practitioners of various forms of meditation.

When you have reached the dreamlike state, there is greater communication between the conscious and unconscious mind. The unconscious mind is able to express—through visual images, metaphors, and dream sequences—the deepest insights of the inner self. Also, when defenses and distractions are at a minimum, the mind is receptive to new kinds of awareness. In the stillness, self-limiting perceptions can be replaced by more positive, expansive attitudes.

The ability to enter this state of deep relaxation at times of your own choosing is invaluable for physical and mental well-being and it is absolutely essential to the success of this program. The finest exercises in Step Two (the Working Dream) would offer little more than the reinforcement of positive attitudes to a person whose brain was in traditional hemispheric balance. To work quickly and effectively with unconscious material, one must allow the analytical self to defer judgment and relinquish leadership during the time that the intuitive self is experiencing the mental imagery.

The Transition from normal consciousness to deep relaxation is easy to learn and extremely satisfying to experience. Mastering this technique will take only as long as you expect it to take. Your mind instructs your central nervous system to relax or to remain tense; it also programs your body to know how long it will take to allow this process to work. Some people require several sessions before they can do it well and others are able to reach a state of deep relaxation within a very few minutes. It's helpful not to try to hurry the process; trying too hard is always counterproductive.

Personal Choices

In choosing the images that will be suggested, I've tried to find the ones most people enjoy. But everyone has certain personal associations that evoke unpleasant memories, so if the images in any exercise in this book are not comfortable for you or helpful to you, choose not to do them—either adjust them to your personal needs or move on to the next experience.

You'll notice that the speech patterns I use while leading you into the Transition are different from an expository pattern. The sentences tend to be longer and instructions are sometimes connected like the cars of a child's train set, hooked together loosely for greater flexibility.

A Means of Transport

Trains are an important image in this program, as you will soon discover. Although for some people they are just a way of getting to work and nothing more, for most of us there are other associations. Trains evoke memories of films of high adventure on the Orient Express, or childhood dreams of magical trips in unknown lands. Trains were among our toys and are woven into our fantasies.

Remember when you were a child, waiting for the train to cross the highway, watching the red flashing of lights, the clanging of the warning bell, the mournful whistle of that machine that came from far in the distance? In your mind's eye, can you see it approaching, feel the vibrations as it passes, count the cars, watch a child wave from the windows, read the names on boxcars if it was a freight? You can listen to the sound of the train passing, listen to the rumbling of the caboose, listen to the sudden presence of silence.

The writer Ray Bradbury loves to ride on trains; in *The Right-Brain Experience* I reported how he gains creative inspiration from the hypnotic sound of the changing scenes that pass by the window as he goes across the country, watching and dreaming and writing. Stories and poems and books are there for the taking as his imagination reaches out into the unfolding landscape to play with a collage of ideas.

In the early stages of this book, I designed an exercise about riding a train and thought it was my own. It was about a magical train that could go where it wanted to go and do what it wanted to do. But soon after that, I read Charles Champlin's column in *The Los Angeles Times* and saw that he too wrote about a magical train in his dreams. It was so much like my own fantasy, it seemed that we had encountered the same dream. A friend observed that this magical train is probably a part of most peoples' childhoods, or at least their dream lives and I think that's true. So perhaps the train runs through the night, from your house to mine and through Bradbury's fantasies and Champlin's dreams and connects us all in a strange sort of fanciful way.

In this program, a train is the means of transport that takes you from your normal state of consciousness through the Transition to the relaxed, dreamlike feeling that is essential for the Working Dream. It is a fine train, moving safely and mysteriously from one reality to another.

Each time you enter the train, your journey will be purposeful. You can ride in your own compartment with your chair next to the window, or you can ride in a glass observation room that is above the height of the engine, so that your view will be unobstructed. The train can have as many or as few cars as you choose. American trains are different from European or Japanese trains, each have their own uniqueness. In my mind, the train is the American variety—noisy, and with a faintly hypnotic sound as it lumbers through the land, with its lights flashing and whistle blowing and the clanging of the wheels on the tracks making a music all its own. If you prefer to adapt that design to make it one that is more appealing to you, please do.

If trains hold no fascination for you, your "train" could be a boat or a plane, a carriage with six white horses, a rocket ship, a glider. It only needs to be a means of transport that does not require your attention for the running of it. You can imagine any changes that will make the process more effective for you; this is your dream and your train and your personal choice, in every step of this program.

Preparation for the Journey

Privacy and quiet are essential while you are learning how to experience Inner Vision techniques. You may need to ask the cooperation of others in the house so that you won't be interrupted.

There are several ways that you can experience these exercises: You can read them first, recall the instructions, and use your memory to carry you through the Dreams. You may prefer to work with a friend and read the exercises for each other in a soft, relaxing voice. (Be sure this is a friend you really trust, for deeply personal material is encountered in the dreams and most people want to reveal what they have experienced.)

Many people enjoy using the professional cassette tapes on which I have recorded the text of the exercises and which may be ordered from:

> Right-Brain Resources, Inc.
> Reseda Medical Building
> 7012 Reseda Blvd., Suite SW 101
> Reseda, CA 91335

Choose the way that seems most appealing to you.

You'll need a pen and a notebook. This notebook will become an extremely personal journal, containing insights both concrete and ephemeral. Part of this Working Dream notebook will reflect the deepest longings from your unconscious mind; part of it will contain practical suggestions for important changes to be made in your life. All of it will reflect the way you are thinking and feeling about yourself and your future.

After you have mastered the ability to enter that deep state of relaxation in just a few moments, you won't need to follow the script for the Transition. But until you're sure that you can make the Transition without the benefit of the relaxation suggestions, it is important not to rush through this critical part of the process.

Following the Transition exercise in this chapter will be a sample of the Working Dream, and the Dreamer and the Critic exercises.

A Word of Precaution

*Never use any of the exercises in this book when your attention is
required by small children or others who are dependent upon your
alertness. These exercises should never be used in a location that
could be dangerous. A person who is emotionally disturbed should
not use these, or any other techniques for dealing with unconscious
material, expect with the help of a professional therapist.*

THE TRANSITION

*This exercise should be used each time you want to experience the
Inner Vision process. It will always precede Step Two (The Working
Dream), and Step Three (The Dreamer and the Critic). Of course,
it can also be used alone, as a technique for inducing deep relaxation. Be sure that you have read the instructions on pages 18–19
before beginning this exercise.*

You are in the place you have chosen as your workroom for
this program, sitting in a comfortable chair, your pen and notebook within easy reach. After you commit this exercise to memory, or listen to a friend's voice, or turn on the cassette tape of the
exercise, close your eyes and enjoy the experience.

Your journey has begun. There is nothing you need to take
with you, for everything that you need has been prepared for you.
If any image is suggested that is not pleasing to you, adjust the
suggestion to meet your personal need.

First, create these images in your mind:

A long, private, deserted beach with golden sand . . .
an ocean with gentle waves . . .
a single set of train tracks running parallel with the shore,
only a short walk from the water's edge.

Beside the tracks, a wooden platform containing a wide
bench, a comfortable chair . . .
between the tracks and the sea, a blanket is spread out on
the sand.

In your fantasy, imagine yourself in this scene. You are waiting for the train that will take you on a magical journey. You have arrived early and may choose to wait on the platform or on the blanket in the sand. You have plenty of time.

Use this time of waiting to begin letting go of the concerns of your daily life.

First, take a deep breath . . . and release it slowly. And then another . . . releasing all tension.

Now breathe normally and be aware of how you are feeling at this moment.

If you brought a great deal of tension with you, acknowledge its presence without criticism. When you are ready to release that tension, you will do so. Take one more deep breath and then exhale any hurtful feelings, any anxieties or tensions, any negative attitudes, for they are of no use to you here.

If distracting thoughts come into your awareness, accept them and let them pass through your mind without drawing your attention from this experience.

Imagine that any negative energy you brought with you is not needed for this journey and, if you want to, you can leave it here. In this relaxation experience, you will decide just how relaxed you want to be.

As much as you are able to do so, concentrate on the "here and now" of this scene: Look at the ocean as if you have never seen it before.

Notice the colors.

Watch one wave and follow it with your attention from far in the distance . . .
notice how it builds . . .
watch when it tumbles to the shore . . .

follow it all the way in . . . luminous and dancing in the sun, it turns to the sea once more.

Watch the clouds . . . the changing forms.

Feel the sun against your body and lie back on the blanket or let the chair recline so that you can stretch out and feel the sun touching you, warming you, pleasing you.

Listen to the sea and hear the distant roar of the waves coming toward the shore. . . . Follow the sound of it to the last whisper of the effervescent bubbles on the sand. Is there a sea gull in the distance? Listen. . . .

Taste your lips and notice the subtle awareness of salt from the sea air.

Take a deep breath and enjoy the cool, refreshing scent of the air.

Feel the sun, warm against your skin. . . . Think of the golden

color of the sun and feel that color on your skin and imagine you can pull it into your lungs and let the healing, soothing energy of the sun fill your body and move all through you, into your shoulders and neck, up into your head, into your thoughts and feelings . . . touching . . . soothing . . . healing . . . feel it moving into your arms . . . hands . . . fingertips . . . into your back . . . along your spine . . . touching . . . soothing . . . healing . . . taking you deeper and deeper into relaxation . . . making you feel good about yourself . . . taking you deeper and deeper . . . moving around your hips and abdomen . . . touching . . . soothing . . . pleasing . . . deeper and deeper into relaxation . . . down your thighs . . . calves . . . ankles . . . down into your feet . . . becoming a positive energy that flows through your body, creating in you the perfect receptiveness for the journey . . . for the train . . . for the Dream.

In the distance, you hear the train approaching. Take your time. . . . The train will stop and wait until you are ready to leave. It is your train and it will be as short or as long as you want it to be and it is coming here just for you and the wonderful journey that is planned for you and you hear the distant whistle. . . . Feel the vibrations in your body as it comes closer . . . and as it approaches it begins to slow.

Hear the sounds of it as it comes gradually to a stop and waits for you.

Observe the train. Notice texture . . . color . . . realize that there is a special place for you to ride that will be the most pleasing to you . . . there is an observation compartment above one of the cars . . . there is a special compartment perhaps, and there are other places you could ride . . . you choose the place that is right for you and settle yourself into that place, observing it carefully. Take time to experience it as being your own. Remember that this "train" will adapt to your needs in any way that you choose and you can adapt the suggestions that follow in any way that seems best for you.

Look out the window at the sea and feel the train rumbling as it begins this journey. Let the train run at whatever speed is most pleasing to you as you watch the changing vista out the window and enjoy the gentle rocking motion . . . the sounds . . . the deeply relaxing sounds of the wheels on steel tracks . . . listen . . . listen . . . listen. . . . Your train is a magical train and it can move on invisible tracks that spread out across the earth, lacing the mountains and the deserts and the plains.

The train can cross continents . . . skim across lakes and seas into distant lands. It can go where it wants to go and do what it wants to do . . .
moving foward in time and backward in time and there is no place in memory or wonderment where your train cannot travel.

The train will carry you to the places that are good for you to go, where you will encounter experiences that are helpful to you. . . .

And the choice is always yours as to how deeply into the dream you will go and how much of the dream you will experience . . .
and the choices you make will always be the choices that are right for you in the Dream.

The train is moving through the vast plains seen in your mind's eye. It moves through the desert where you see the dry sands and desert flowers and tumbleweeds springing like rabbits on a summer day. It moves on through changing vistas. And you feel very comfortable with the speed of the train, for it seems to reflect the speed of your thoughts and the energy in your body. The train continues at this speed for a while, until you notice that gradually the train moves slower and slower still, then even slower, still reflecting the rhythm established by your body and your mind. Listen to the cadence of the sounds and concentrate on the clicking and the clacking of the wheels on the steel tracks. Let the train move at any speed it chooses, knowing that it will carry you safely along on your journey and you can feel relaxed and even more relaxed. Notice the steady, even pattern of your breathing and the same rhythmical pattern of the sound of the wheels moving along the tracks. Now it doesn't matter whether the train moves quickly or slowly for the rhythm of your breathing is just right for you and everything that happens to you on this journey will be good for you and you can relax and go deeper and deeper into the good feelings you are experiencing now.

Soon the train moves in slow motion, as in a dream.
And you are entering the Dream.

Notice that there is a soft fog pressing against the window . . . the fog is part of the Dream, as you are part of the Dream.

The train slows now, and stops. . . .
Walk from your seat to the steps . . .
down the steps to the platform . . .
into the soft fog. . . .

Follow the path made of cobblestones or bricks which leads you through the fog into a new experience.

THE WORKING DREAM

Discovering Your Powers

The path you have chosen will lead you into a warm and exquisite land. It is a land of dreams and mystery. There is a bridge that will lead you over to this magical land, where you have greater powers than you ever realized before. Cross the bridge any way you choose—you could walk . . . or run . . . or ride. You could float as in a dream.

> Look around you and notice what you see—the colors, the textures. Be aware of the scent in the air and the sounds your feet make on the path.

In this place you are not bound by convention or by gravity or by anything at all. . . . You are free to do whatever it pleases you to do, whatever is good for you to do.

> You are in a wonderful place that is beautiful to see and where only good things will happen to you. Perhaps there are many trees in this place. . . .
> Notice the color and the texture . . . be aware of the sounds.

Explore the land in your own way and find that it is good. Notice the sky above you and take time to watch the changing shape of the clouds.

> This is a place to test your powers. To discover that you can bring forth anything you want by the powers of your imagination.

Let something wonderful appear before you now . . . something that is alive . . . something you could only create in a dream. See this living creature vividly before you.

> Listen as it speaks to you now. And let the words that you hear reveal something that is important for you to know.

You can say anything you want to say. . . .

> And you can hear anything that you want to hear.

You can get to know this dream-character in any way that pleases you, any way that is good for you.

> And there is something important that you can learn from this experience that will have great meaning to you in the future.

Stay with the Dream as long as it is good for you to do so. . . .

> Take your time.

Remember, you have all the power you need to help you enjoy the Dream.

> When you are ready to return to your workroom, let your thoughts move slowly and easily back to that room and just as you move from a sleeping dream into the twilight state of wakefulness and then to alert awareness, you can awaken from the Working Dream in that same way.

THE DREAMER AND THE CRITIC

In your notebook for the Working Dream, write down what you felt and what you saw. Be as specific as you can be, for each detail in your association to your Dream has meaning. You may want to write the names of the characters, or the events, or your feelings in your notebook, in any order that they occur to you. Write down any associations you have to the Dream, for even the most subtle images can be important and are worthy of your attention. Did you meet someone who was helpful, or who presented new insights to you about any situation in your life? If so, make careful notes about what was revealed to you.

Of course, all the images and thoughts, feelings and suggestions that came to you in the Dream were created by your unconscious mind to help you understand yourself with greater clarity and insight.

The Dreamer and the Critic is an important third step in the Inner Vision process. It helps you use the analytical powers of the left hemisphere of your brain to balance the intuitive insights you encountered in the Dream. Although the Dreamer helps you gain perspective on your situation, it is the good Critic from your left hemisphere that helps you to evaluate your insights and perceptions.

Although The Working Dream has ended, it may take a few minutes to regain the full analytical powers of your left hemisphere. (Just as, first thing in the morning, you need a few minutes to become fully alert.) You may want to return to the Dreamer and the Critic at a later time to consider the suggestions of your Critic. If you want to reenter quickly, try adding a column of numbers or alphabetizing a few dozen words. Some people claim that they can "feel the shift" from Dreamer to Critic.

Personal Stories

It's helpful to discover how others use the three steps of the Inner Vision process to reveal their personal insights. Sometimes the Dreams and their interpretations bring new awareness, at other times they reinforce what you already know to be true. Occasionally they are powerful, confronting you with the depths of your feelings. Often they are playful, but their lightheartedness shouldn't be a measure of their importance.

Even the Transition exercise, which was designed only as a technique for relaxation, can be used to invoke insights if one pays attention to the metaphors that emerge. Helen Pankowsky, M.D., one of the psychiatrists in the control group that tested the exercises in this book, realized that her chair on the train was turned in such a way that she could only see backwards. She had to move to another location on the train before she was able to see what was before her. Helen was quick to point out to the group that it was a perfect metaphor for how she had been responding to her recent move to California: Every new experience in Los Angeles had caused her to look backward to her past and make comparisons with a very different culture. Until confronted by the metaphor her unconscious mind selected, she was unaware of how this "backward perspective" had prevented her from seeing the full range of possibilities in her new home.

Sometimes seminar participants visualize their personal train as a plane, a spaceship, or one of various other modes of transportation. Remember that with all of these suggestions for the Working Dream, you are the one who creates the vision that is right for you.

Choosing Your Dreams

The Dream you just experienced is a very simple Working Dream. Its only purpose was to stir your imagination and help you realize that you can create anything you want to create in Dreams. In the Working Dreams that follow, you will be addressing specific issues, but in this first Dream, nothing was required of you but to play with the imagery in any way that pleased you.

Every chapter in this book is designed to give you a powerful tool for altering perception and seeing the possibilities for your future. Inner Vision techniques will provide the structure for your visions—it is up to you to invent your future through the Dreams.

CHAPTER 3

CLAIMING YOUR
POWER

———◆———

Every man bears throughout every moment of his life the responsibility for what he will make of the next hour, or how he will
shape the next day. During no moment of his life does man
escape the mandate to choose among possibilities.

Those challenging words weren't written by some idealistic phi-
losopher sitting safely in his ivory tower; they were wrenched from
the pain and wisdom of Dr. Viktor Frankl, who was a prisoner in
the concentration camps at Auschwitz and Dachau. In his book,
The Doctor and the Soul, after describing the psychological patterns of prisoners in the concentration camps, Dr. Frankl wrote:

For whatever may have been taken from them in their first hour
in camp—until his last breath no one can wrest from a man his
freedom to take one or another attitude toward his destiny. And
alternative attitudes really did exist.

Alternative attitudes exist for all of us, and alternative actions,
as well. In spite of the influence of circumstances and the behavior
of others, we invent our own futures by the sum of our reactions,
attitudes, and actions. Through the power of our perceptions, we

have the ability to *choose* how we will respond to any circumstance.

The press coverage of various incidents of terrorism has shown us that hostages have revealed a variety of responses to their situations. Like the prisoners in the concentration camps, all hostages experienced fear and anxiety, for there is no other normal reaction to being held captive. But during their ordeals, each responded to the situation in his or her own unique way: Some allowed the circumstances to define them as victims, and they sought no reservoirs of inner strength to help them take any kind of positive action. Others took charge of their fears and adjusted their perspective. One of the hostages in the 1985 Beirut hijacking incident tried to understand his captors' motivations and deal constructively with them. He made an effort to perceive the situation from their perspective and even had compassion for the people whose actions he deplored. Many people in America, however, misunderstood his attitude, perhaps because of their own inability to evaluate that situation from another perspective.

In every important situation in your life, your response is determined by three factors:

- *Your reaction:* Your reaction is how you *feel* about your situation; it is instinctive, emotional, and immediate.

- *Your attitude:* Your attitude is the way you *view* your situation; it may be altered by perception.

- *Your actions:* Your action is what you *do* about your situation; it may be the result of assigning your power to others or of claiming responsibility for your choices. Actions are influenced strongly by perception.

Your response is composed of your reaction, your attitude, and your actions.

REJECTING THE ROLE OF VICTIM

No person on earth is exempt from the possibility of facing circumstances that are devastating, and the option of accepting the role of victim, survivor, or victor. Knowing that you have a choice is the first step in exerting conscious control over your future. The story that follows involves a brutal act and a courageous response. It is a story of bravery and an example of how neither circumstance nor the violent behavior of others can destroy someone who rejects the role of victim and takes responsibility for his or her own responses.

You might think the girl in my office was innocent of life's harsher realities, if you were to judge by the standards we use for quick assessment: confident body language, obvious pride in her appearance, strength behind the softness of voice, a lilt in the gentle laugh that seems a quiet celebration of life. We met two years ago, only a few weeks after she survived an attack that tested every inner resource. Her story is included in this book, with permission, because the courage she developed through months of emotional recovery may benefit others who have been victimized.

On a quiet Sunday afternoon, three men forced their way into her San Francisco apartment, held a gun to her husband's head—threatening to kill him and their baby if she resisted—and raped her in ways that I will not describe. She did as she was told, and her baby and husband were not physically harmed.

There are many factors that contributed to her emotional survival in the months that followed. There were people who loved and comforted her. A therapist listened while she talked through the terrifying memories and the recurring nightmares. I suggested positive imagery that helped her build self-esteem. Her husband, however, was not one of those who helped her to recover. Unable to cope with his own feelings about what was done to her that night, he divorced her within a few months of the attack.

She chose to take charge of her future.

Those who were available to help her could have accomplished nothing if she had not decided to help herself. The choice was hers and she chose wisely.

First, she acknowledged her feelings. There was no denial of the rage and hatred, the sense of degradation. She feared the night terrors that came when she slept and she feared the challenges of the day when her own personal resources were so fragile. She was afraid of the future and the vividness of memories from the past. But she never tried to deny the depth of her feelings, acknowledging that grief was a necessary part of the healing process.

She took responsibility for her attitude. While accepting her reactions, she began to work on her attitude toward what had happened. She decided that, although she would move to a different apartment, she would not live in fear of another attack. She would choose to deal constructively with her feelings. Hatred toward the rapists and bitterness toward her husband would only turn back on her as destructive forces, as hurtful in her life as the acts that had caused her trouble. Emotions that had been appropriate at first were preventing her from moving forward with her life. She chose to claim power over her attitudes, to use the negative emotions to lead her toward constructive actions.

She chose to take responsibility for her actions. She refused to remain a victim, and took positive actions for the future. When the rapists were caught, she faced them in court and was able to testify before the judge, the jury, and a room full of indifferent strangers. It was a painful but important and self-affirming act. The men were convicted with maximum sentences, and she began to "let go" of the memories.

Sometimes, people can't avoid being victimized by circumstances or by other people—but no one has to remain a victim to his or her own responses.

It is important to understand that the inmates of the concentration camps, the hostages, and the abused young woman are all extreme examples chosen to show how claiming one's own power can influence the future—no matter how painful the past. (As stated earlier, the exercises in this book should not be used to deal with the memory of physical or psychological violence unless a psychiatrist or clinical psychologist is supervising the imagery session.)

These three examples provide a touchstone: If people can choose to exercise their own power in those extreme situations, why should you and I make less courageous choices in taking charge of our own lives?

Taking Charge

It can be helpful to each of us to occasionally evaluate our lives and to consider who has been making the important choices. Some choices are made by circumstance; some choices are made when we allow others to make our personal decisions for us. The most responsible choices are those we make for ourselves.

Of course, not all of our choices will fit neatly into these tidy categories, and those of us who want life to be black or white often have difficulty coping with the shades of gray that color most situations. Still, there is value in recognizing the predominant forces that influence our decisions as we consider the option of exercising greater control over our lives.

HIGHER CHOICES

Making our own choices doesn't imply selfishness. We may make choices against what we want for ourselves in favor of what our children want, or of what we want for our children. We may choose a course that is not the one we would prefer if our priority is to please someone we love. And we may make choices against fulfilling our immediate personal desires for the sake of higher values—but we make those decisions deliberately, not because there is no choice to make.

CHOICES MADE BY CIRCUMSTANCE

Some situations are assigned to you in life. You had no choice about who your parents would be, or whether they would be loving or unkind. You had no choice as to whether you would grow up in wealth or in poverty or in the middle class, in one country or another, of one race or another, exposed to the attitudes of one religion or another. You were born with an aptitude for certain skills and talents; your intelligence potential and your physical appearance were built into your genes.

These are "the givens." That's the way it was. But very early in life, you began to exert your will to make decisions about what you would do with your "basic assignment." Some children know when they are very young that they will make choices to change their lives, yet there are adults who have never realized that they have options.

CHOICES MADE BY OTHERS

I'll tell you a parable about a young man who wanted to be an artist. He had talent and tenacity and was willing to live simply to follow his dream. But the young man was quite tied to his dominating mother and fearful of the disapproval of his father, who had little patience with his artistic dreams. He was in love with a young woman whose parents were not only anxious for them to marry, but also wanted him to come into the family business, which was highly lucrative. Well, there you have it: a young man's moment of choice.

Years later, when the blush of love had faded and he found himself wedded not only to his wife, but to all the encumbrances of her wealth, he said there had really been no choice to make at all. *No one could pass up such an opportunity*, he said of his new appointment as president of the firm—but his voice seemed as flat and colorless as a blank canvas.

When we allow others to make our decisions for us, or to manipulate us into making the decisions they want us to make, we must still acknowledge that we are choosing to abdicate our power.

Are there choices you allowed others to make for you that you wish you had made for yourself? And are there choices you chose *not* to make, or avoided making so that you would not feel accountable for the decision? If so, the Working Dream will help you get in touch with some of those situations and consider what positive action can be taken now. It will also help you understand whether you have really been in charge of your life and enable you to acknowledge your possibilities for the future.

CHOICES MADE FOR YOURSELF

Making responsible choices often involves consulting with others for their insights and expert opinions. There is no reason to exclude the wisdom of other sources you have learned to trust and admire, but it is essential that you acknowledge your own responsibility for the final decision.

Even the great religious leaders throughout history, who have sought their counsel from the Highest Power, have ultimately had to interpret their prayerful insights through their own understanding. And the choices they have made, however inspired, were nonetheless their own.

When you take responsibility for your choices and are willing to accept the credit or the consequences for your attitudes and actions, you join that small group of people in the world who are mastering their lives. Perhaps you are already there. Or perhaps you are considering whether you even want that responsibility. For now, I hope you will at least acknowledge that at every moment there are options, and you can accept, assign, or abdicate responsibility for the important decisions in your life.

Be Good to Yourself

If you are feeling hard on yourself about past decisions, realize that you did the best you could on any given day, considering the information you had, your emotional strength, and your personal insights. No matter how you try, you can't remake the past. You can, however, explore ways to alter your perceptions about your present situation, and from this moment forward determine to design for yourself a more fulfilling future.

Aldous Huxley expressed his thoughts on the potential of personal choice in rich and powerful imagery:

The choice is always ours. Then, let me choose . . .
Cherishingly to tend and feed and fan
That inward fire, whose small precarious flame,
Kindled or quenched, creates
The noble or the ignoble men we are,
The worlds we live in and the very fates,
Our bright or muddy star.

THE TRANSITION

*Remember: You need your Working Dream notebook . . . a pen
. . . a quiet place. Remember the series of events that will carry you
into Transition as you close your eyes and experience again: a quiet
beach . . . ocean sounds . . . the colors . . . the deep relaxation
. . . your personal train . . . invisible tracks moving through space
and through time. (Experience the feelings through memory or by
reading again pages 19–24.)*

THE WORKING DREAM

Over, Under, Around, or Through

*Your private train carried you into a relaxed, receptive, dreamlike
state where your unconscious mind can express itself through the
images and visions of the Working Dream. Your Dream Maker (that
part of yourself that creates each character and scene in these experiences) will reveal important truths to you in mysterious, evocative
ways.*

The small station is located in a place you have never been to
before but which you know is a good place and a safe place for you
to be. You are high in the mountains, and you don't see anyone
there, nor do you expect anyone, for this journey is a private one,
for you alone.

You walk through the fog into the sunlight, feel the warmth of
it touching your face, and the smell of the air is clean and fresh.

> As you follow the path that leads into a forest, you realize
> that you will come home a different way, and you no longer
> need your train on this journey. . . . Listen to the sound
> of it, moving on. Know that only good experiences are
> ahead of you.

You are aware of the color of the trees and the texture of the bark
on the trees, the smell of pine and of plants that grow only in this
place and that refresh you with their fragrance.

On this journey, there is someone you are going to meet and something you will discover, and the experience will give you insights that are important.

Notice that to the side of the trail the ground drops to a lower level. . . . From your vantage point you can see that on that lower level, which is quite a way down, there is a fence—and it reminds you of a high fence around a child's playground. The size of the enclosure is about the size of an average backyard in an average neighborhood, but there are no houses here, only the mountains and the trees, the clouds and forest creatures.

In the playground, there is a small child who seems to be looking for a way to get out.

No one is with the child, which strikes you as odd and causes you to wonder how the child got there.

From your position, high above, you can clearly see that there is a way the child could have gotten in and a way that the child could get out.

On one side of the fence is rich meadow grass, with several trails crossing nearby. . . . On the other side of the playground there is a deep lake that reaches to touch the very edge of the fencing that encloses the playground.

Right beside you there is a slide which is rather steep but inviting and the metal slide is the longest one you have ever seen, and it stretches from where you are standing to the middle of the playground.

Since you are curious about the child, and wonder if it needs your help, you take the trip down the slide to the grassy place, and you feel the warm metal slide against your legs, all the way down the slide.

When you come to the bottom, your feet touch the thick, green grass that covers the playground.

The child has watched you take the trip down the slide.

"Who are you?" the child wonders, and you might say your name, or that your are a friend, or that you are on a journey to discover who you really are and perhaps you can answer that question better at a later time.

You may want to ask the child the same question, "Who are you?" and the child may or may not give you a specific answer, but it doesn't matter. For now you realize that the child is sad and trying very hard to hold back tears, and you want to comfort the child and to find out what could cause such sadness in this beautiful place.

And then the child tells you of feelings of being helpless and afraid and wondering where to go next and how to get out of this space with the high fence, and the child wonders if there is a way out at all.

And you take time to listen to the child's fears and to give comfort, being careful to honor the child's honest reactions.

You promise to help and you reassure the child that there is a way out which will be found, if you work together and try to discover other perspectives.

And you have no fear, for yourself or the child, because you know that you will find the way out at the proper time.

There are many things for the child to learn that cannot be learned unless you both work together.

Tell the child that anything that you wish for will appear in the area if it will help you out of your predicament. But then quickly suggest that what you might hope for is not simply a shovel or a ladder, for while that would be functional, it would be no fun at all—for what's the good of going through the forest if you create only ordinary solutions to your problems?

The child will imagine a possibility and then you will imagine a possibility and so on, until the child reaches the best creative solution.

And now the child makes the first suggestion—that you could get out of the enclosure by wishing for a rabbit and a large, friendly dog. The rabbit might scurry down into a small hole under the fence and the dog, trying to catch the rabbit, would dig and dig and dig until the hole would be large enough for you and the child to slip through.

And then you might suggest that you could get out by wishing for a trampoline that you could place near the side of the fence, and you could spring so high that you could fling yourself over the fence and into the lake and then swim to shore.

And then what do you suggest? Write it down.

And then what does the child suggest? Write it down.

And is there more to consider and more to be said?

When the child has learned that there are many options to a problem, and has reached the best solution, you are ready to leave the playground. The solution may be very complicated or it may be quite simple. The choice is up to you and the child.

The child is happy now, and sure of the way home, as you are sure of the path that leads you on your journey. If there is something you want to say to the child, say it now, as you go your separate ways.

At the edge of the lake, you sit down to consider what you have experienced in the Working Dream. What were you feeling in the enclosure? Write about these feelings in your Working Dream notebook.

What was the child feeling? And you write that down also. Is there something about the child that reminds you of yourself? Write down your answer and your associations to the question.

Now the dream is ending and it's time to think about returning to your workroom. . . .

Now you are moving through the twilight from altered consciousness to wakefulness. . . . You return to your usual world just as each morning you pass from darkness to light, from dreams to consciousness.

Now you are in your workroom and when you are ready, open your eyes and consider the journey you have just taken. Make any notes that are important to you and move on to the next phase of this experience.

THE DREAMER AND THE CRITIC

The insights that you have written in your notebook have come with the help of your inner Dream Maker; they reveal your fears and longings, wishes and hopes. Dream Makers draw some excellent ideas from your unconscious mind, but sometimes the good ideas get mixed up with magical longings, and that's why this next part of the experience is very important. *You must never act on the insights of your right-brain experience without first testing them against the analytical evaluations of your logical left brain.* Mature decisions are made by balancing the insights and judgment of both hemispheres of your brain.

Now that the dream has ended, evaluate what you learned from the child. Do these insights seem valuable to the logical, analytical part of yourself. How does this understanding contribute to solving whatever problems you are now working through in your own life?

What habit patterns occur to you when you think about springing out of trouble on a trampoline or by using other people (animals, in this case) to do your work for you? In the solutions suggested by you and the child, is there any metaphor that hints at the ways you usually deal with problems? (For example, a woman who imagined the fence was made of tall candy-canes realized that she often tried to eat her way out of her problems.)

Sometimes a child who is vulnerable reminds us of our own inner child who dwells in each of us all of our lives. That vulnerable part of ourselves needs to be nurtured and needs to be comforted at certain times. There isn't a king or queen or president who has not experienced such a feeling of loneliness and helplessness. We are all fragile sometimes, and it is the strong and capable among us who are least afraid to acknowledge the inner child.

Do you see how the positive attitude you brought to the child can be helpful to your own inner child and to your understanding of some situation in your life? Do you need to be more comforting to your inner child or does your inner child need to be more attentive to your adult strength? Perhaps both things are true. What do you think?

Perhaps the child slid into the grassy area through circumstance (maybe the plan was only to sit at the top of the slide and then the "accident" happened). Perhaps the child followed the advice of another, knowing better, but "going along" and then got into difficulty. Perhaps the child chose the adventurous way and then was overwhelmed. Perhaps there is some truth in all of these possibilities.

What is important to remember is that no matter what got the child into the difficult situation, it was the child's responsibility to either find a way out or ask help from someone who could add another perspective to the problem. It was still ultimately up to the child to make the decision to solve the problem and claim the power of personal responsibility.

All the characters in a Working Dream represent some part of yourself (just as characters in nighttime dreaming are fragments of your total personality). If you want to, you can choose to learn a great deal about yourself from your dream characters.

What is about to happen in your own life as a result of these insights is strictly up to you.

Personal Stories

When you read how three participants responded to this one Working Dream, you will realize that my suggestions only provide the stage upon which the Dreamers enact their own unique stories. They created the characters, the emotions, and interactions, and the interpretations that enabled them to gain insights from the Dream. You meet them now for the first time, but you will get to know more about them, and about others who participated in the control groups, as we move through the experiences.

Jay Myers, Ph.D., is a psychobiologist who received his doctorate from Cal Tech; he spent several years conducting studies on "split-brain" patients whose unique problems have helped scientists better understand the functions of the left and the right sides of the brain. Jay has published several scientific papers on the subject of brain lateralization, working in collaboration with Nobel Laureate Dr. Roger Sperry. When I wrote *The Right-Brain Experience*, Jay was one of my first readers and provided valuable insights that enhanced the material. When he agreed to shift his position from objective scientist to subjective Dreamer, I knew that his contributions would be invaluable once again.

Jay moved easily from his pleasurable experience on the train to the Working Dream. When he came to the slide, he immediately wanted to slip down into the playground. Jay's solution for how to get out of the enclosure was to imagine the fence was built of a complex structure of mirrors which allowed him to perceive his position in such a way that he was standing on the *outside* of the fence. I would have thought that this analytical approach would pull him out of the Dream, but Jay pointed out that he didn't consciously design the fence so much as he *experienced* the fence in its completion and just observed its elaborate construction. He remained in a deep, dreamlike state throughout the experience.

The child, whom Jay recognized as his own inner child, had a different way of approaching the problem and it was the child's solution that captivated Jay's attention. The child imagined that the fence was made of matchsticks—actually, they appeared as *matchstick people* with faces and arms encircling each other to create the fence. The child's solution for getting out of the enclosure was to run toward the fence yelling *fire* and waving a flame so that the match-stick people were frightened and fled in all directions.

Jay was having fun with the dream and when he wrote his association in the Dreamer and the Critic, he realized how his adult self had created a complicated solution while the child had provided a simple, effective one. Jay seemed amused to realize that the child projected his feelings of anxiety onto the fence; so instead of the boy feeling afraid it was the *fence* that felt afraid, and then it was the boy who had the power!

At first, Jay didn't see the full implications of the Dream. But that night while sleeping he dreamed that he was a child and the child had started a fire that was raging out of control. When we met again, he talked about the sleeping dream and Jay began to see that the fire was a metaphor for other things that were out of control in his life. His first child had been born a few months before, and he was feeling the traditional pressures: not enough time for his baby, not enough time for his wife, not enough time for his research . . . and perhaps there was the unspoken awareness that there was not enough time for Jay.

Jay found that it was extremely helpful to confront the intensity of his feelings. Both the Working Dream and his sleeping dream provided effective catalysts to put him in touch with what was out of control within himself.

Jay has not yet arrived at a solution, but at least he has clearly defined the problem. Now he sees that he must begin to change either his expectations or his situation.

If you watched the Summer Olympics in 1984, you'll remember the spectacular opening ceremonies. It was Broadway choreographer and three-time Tony Award winner Ron Field who was responsible for much of what you saw that evening. He choreographed those dancers and athletes and politicians with the same creative skills he used to choreograph the musicals *Cabaret* and *Applause* and *Peter Pan*. Ron also has a couple of Emmys to his credit and has created dances for just about every dancing star around—from Fred Astaire and Gene Kelly to Michael Jackson and Baryshnikov. He is obviously a man who has known how to gain access to the powers of his imagination for a very long time. But like many high achievers, he is always receptive to ideas that can help him develop even more of his innate resources.

I worked with Ron for the first time in 1983 and led him through a series of mental exercises to stimulate right-brain thinking. Then he asked me to work with the dancers in the musical *Merlin*, using imagery to establish a bonding and a supportive atmosphere among them. In 1985, Ron began using my tapes to enhance his imaging abilities and while listening to them, he would often visualize what he wanted to create in a show. He and I are working more closely now, while Ron is developing a unique concept in dance theater, called "Soundstage 10." He is the first to say that there are many risks involved in any project that is revolu- tionary in style—and that requires millions of dollars to produce. But he's not afraid to take responsibility for his decisions, win or lose. This Working Dream reveals his attitude toward personal power during a time of high stress.

The private session began with Ron telling me about the heavy responsibility he feels for the performers and the investors in his show.

In the Dream, when Ron went down the slide, he had the sensation of entering a safe and protected studio where wonderful things could be performed. He had no apprehension about being locked in; he felt a freeing sensation, as if the world and all of its pressures could be locked out for a while. He immediately recog- nized the boy, whom he called "Ronnie," as his inner child and experienced good feelings about seeing him so clearly. He had a strong awareness that Ronnie needed to feel more playful, and to enjoy this beautiful place where there was no factor of risk.

Ron spent a long time just enjoying the "studio." He focused on how vulnerable the child was, as all children are, to the realities of the outside world. He felt protective of that child and of "all the other children who want so much to succeed and need someone to help them discover how."

The child had no fear in the playground and allowed himself to trust Ron without reservation. Neither of them wanted to leave the "studio." When I suggested that it was time to find a way out, he thought of flying (which is something he often does when I lead him in dreams), but he quickly realized that he simply didn't want to go—and in dreams (as is often true in life) when you don't want to do something, you find a way to control the outcome. Ron and Ronnie had every intention of resisting the suggestion to leave. Ronnie thought of dancing out, but Ron knew that even Baryshni- kov couldn't do a *grand plié* high enough to spring over that fence.

They agreed to stay where they were and enjoy it. Ron invited others to come to the studio and he and Ronnie entertained them and helped them learn to dance. He felt good about their trust and knew that he would not disappoint them. Even though he wasn't sure how to get out of the enclosure, *he knew that he would have the solution when he needed it*. In the meantime, Ron was enjoying himself with those who had put themselves into his care. And, just as he suspected, when he felt it was time to leave, he led them out by simply commanding the fence to let them through—and it did!

We talked about the Dream immediately after the experience, and Ron focused on the awareness that he was comfortable with the amount of responsibility he has assumed. The weight was not too heavy.

Because Ron felt so exquisitely happy when he experienced the presence of the child, he had a strong revelation that even if he does feel like "caretaker of the world" much of the time, Ron Field must make time to nurture his inner child.

Ron's resistance to leaving the playground is not unusual; in fact, you will probably resist a suggestion or two, as I lead you into the various Dreamscapes. Always go with your instincts; if I suggest flying and you want to swim, by all means, swim. The Dreams, as I suggest them, set the stage for one type of experience, but if you choose to have another, it may be because your inner advisor is leading you to a different discovery. You are the one who knows what is best for you. Trust the wisdom of your inner advisor.

When I first met Barbara Sax, M.D., I remember thinking that if ever there was a Superwoman, here she was. Barbara was a radiologist before she changed her specialty—now she is a psychiatrist who works with inpatients at a Los Angeles mental health facility. She now has a full schedule at the hospital, although in the past she has taken seasons off occasionally to attend to family commitments—she has seven children, the youngest of whom is twelve. If those facts don't convince you that we have here a most unusual woman, let me add the clincher: Tall and stunning in soft lavender silk, she came to our second imagery session with a gift of home-baked bread that she had made that very morning. She also has a terrific sense of humor, which, considering the complexity of her life, I suppose one must cultivate or perish.

The exercise in this chapter was the one I led that first day when Barbara came to my home with the others in her control group. She was very quiet after this Working Dream, revealing only that the Dream was more powerful and evoked much more primitive emotion than she had expected. She didn't volunteer the content of the Dream and I didn't ask, hoping that she would reveal her experience in her own time. Later, she wrote me a letter about the Dream and her associations to it. Because she writes about the experience so effectively, this description will be in her own words, using the present tense, as I recommend that you do when recalling Dreams, for it enhances their vividness.

Thursday morning, 3:30 AM.

I chose to experience The Working Dream again, just now. I am amazed, incredulous and shocked at the strength of these feelings. I am flushed and very warm. When I was doing the exercise at your house, I experienced much of these same feelings, but I was too intimidated at the time even to allow myself any detail of what was going on. . . . I wasn't expecting this exercise to be so powerful—not the first time, and not now, as I read the exercise in your manuscript. By previous experience, imagery had never been particularly powerful for me. Interesting, yes—but not this!

Here it is then, my notes, my feelings about the Dream and the Dream Revisited:

Moving away from my train, floating really, through the mauve fog which is a pleasant and reassuring extension of my train, into the warm sunlight and fragrant green forest, I feel a sense of peace and delighted tingling anticipation of the adventure ahead. A rude surprise, then, this spasm of gut-pain, fear actually, which clutches me as I catch view of the slide leading into a prison-like enclosure.

It reminds me of a sleeping-dream I experienced some months ago. In that dream, I was imprisoned, I could see no light, no opening. And in that dream too, the door was there, not locked as I had "known" but unlatched, waiting simply to be opened.

Recalling the sleeping-dream, I hesitate. I don't have to go down the slide, I don't have to continue the Dream, I have choices and I can choose to pull back, to create other images, to resist the suggested imagery. But I am drawn to this setting, and want—no, *need* to go down that slide into the place where the child waits.

I choose to be in the enclosure with the child, and find that I am enveloped in a cloak of panic: I have the entire responsibility to get the child (and myself) out of that cell. I know without looking that the child's face is tear-stained, her eyes pleading to me to effect her escape. The child and I have a serious obstacle to overcome. I can still hear your voice, the comforting and encouraging tones about this adventure, but the playful approach feels intrusive and irritatingly distracting. Within the dream, I am aware that this is, indeed, 'only' a dream . . . and yet, I cannot shake my discomfort, my anxiety. I feel exclusively responsible for the success of this 'mission' but lack the necessary knowledge and skills, and am too frightened to entertain any playful creative alternatives. At the last, I move toward a gate which I had seen there all along and assumed to be bolted shut. But now I see the logical solution: simply to open the unlocked gate. We walk out together, the child's sweaty little hand in mine. We are not skipping or singing.

In the Dreamer and the Critic, I am reminded that when I struggle with feelings of being controlled, trapped, imprisoned in life, I give free rein to that frightened impotent inner child; my functional adult needs to look at options, but the inner child, instead, for too long a moment, takes charge. Or rather, cannot take charge. Perhaps, too, I create my own locked doors.

And so you see, this 'working dream' had become serious business for me. The child had looked to me, the adult, for her escape—but I was the child too. Many metaphors. The Critic came running in to rescue me with good intellectual thinking.

Remembering now . . . my inner-child, who felt so overwhelmed by her Pavarotti-esque but also very critical father, once more becomes the adult in order to protect her mother who seemed too weak to tolerate her father's scary power. Whether fact or fiction, this belief was cast in stone for the child and reemerges, distressingly, unexpectedly, as it did today. I was the child who needed to accompany her father and please him in ways which seemed impossible but necessary, in order to protect my mother whose vulnerability seemed my special responsibility to protect. A terribly adult responsibility for a small child. I feel overwhelmed. Perhaps I don't have to do this for her, but I cannot leave her to try to survive his ebullience and irritable energy alone. Was it only in my fantasy I had to take on this responsibility.

I consider again my earlier statement: 'Perhaps I create my own locked doors.'

Now I reflect on the section of this chapter of Higher Choices. Must higher choices necessarily imply that only the 'other'—family, husband, child, whatever—be given consideration? I rail at

the notion that giving validity to the needs of the self is, by impli-
cation, a 'lower' choice . . . that responsibility to others is the
'higher choice' and it is selfish to include oneself in the decision.
Is it not true that responsibility needs to include consideration of
oneself, and that 'higher choice' may be validly a selfish one?

The Dream was challenging and valuable to Barbara for obvious reasons. It is valuable to us to assess how others use the
Dreamscape, to feel their experience, as well as our own. Remember that Barbara made the choice to go down the slide and enter
the nightmare her unconscious mind invited her to experience—
and to learn from. She could also have chosen not to go down that
slide, or even, once there, to stop the Dream.

A MATTER OF CHOICE

When we are asleep, we have no conscious choice of what dreams
we will entertain. In the Working Dream, the choice is always
there for us to make.

The Dreams in this book have been designed as gentle encounters to lead you in the most positive direction you can imagine. But
if there is any doubt in your mind as to whether you want to enter
a specific Dreamscape or envision a suggested image, read it over
first so that there will be no surprises.

Imagine that a banquet table has been set with an abundance
of delicious choices. Avoid what you may be allergic to—and enjoy everything that is satisfying and pleasurable to experience.

The Dreamscape in this chapter is one of the most emotionally
challenging of all the Inner Vision exercises, for it invites us to
claim responsibility for our situations. There is no suggested script
for blaming others, and there is no one to make our decisions for
us. For Jay, the Dreamscape was a playful experience which was
only the first step in his realization that it was time to draw the line
and change his attitude or his situation. For Ron, the Dreamscape
provided an escape from the pressures of his work, reinforcing his
strengths, indicating that he is comfortable with the degree of
responsibility he has chosen. And Barbara used the Dreamscape to
encounter the realization that she needs to stop creating locked

doors for herself. She is also evaluating the possibility that she takes on more responsibility for others than is healthy for her to assume.

Whether you worked in the Dreamscape with playful images or with serious ones, know that all messages from your Dream Maker are valuable and worthy of your attention.

It is one thing to recognize the metaphors of your Dream Maker and quite another thing to take action on the insights that come to you during the Dream. If you really want to make changes in your future, you will need to consider your new awarenesses carefully, and then decide which of them should be applied to your life.

CHAPTER 4

KNOWING WHO YOU ARE—KNOWING WHAT YOU WANT

◆

Psychological questionnaires designed to help us understand ourselves better have appeared in popular magazines and self-help books for years. It is as if we believe that the questions addressed to our innermost thoughts and feelings will hold a mirror before our psyches and reflect hidden aspects of our personalities. So we check the boxes showing what is "true" and what is "false" and we make lists of the situations that cause us to feel confident or vulnerable, depressed or happy, guilty or lonely or bored.

There's nothing wrong with the questions that help us identify our feelings—it's just that they are being asked of the wrong hemisphere of the brain. None of us can answer those questions with emotional honesty if we confront them when all our defenses are working. When our strong, healthy egos have a chance to run interference and defend our vulnerable feelings, we are protected from important aspects of the truth. No matter how well-meaning we are, the guard who watches the door to the secrets we keep from ourselves isn't about to hand over the key that easily.

But if you ask these questions of your right brain when you have moved through the Transition to the Dreamscape (while your guard isn't paying much attention), you'll discover answers that may surprise you with the perceptions they reveal. It's best if the questions are not asked in direct, confrontational sentences (at least not at first), for the unconscious mind resists the direct approach and will often refuse to play the game on these terms. In the Working Dream, you can project your feelings onto the screen of your mind's eye and discover your personal metaphors without resistance.

THE MIRROR THAT REFLECTS FEELINGS

Did you ever confront a little girl who wouldn't tell you why she was crying, and no amount of questioning would bring forth the answer? But if you distracted her thoughts from her own situation and asked her why her doll was sad, she probably gave you an explanation. And soon you knew what the little girl was feeling. Even if the child didn't know why she felt so unhappy, you would probably have a pretty good clue, if you knew how to listen for the metaphors in what she said about her doll.

I know a chief executive officer of a billion-dollar firm who responded well to a technique that's actually not any more complicated than that one. He is a powerful man whose pride prevented him from telling anyone (even himself) how threatened he felt of losing control—but he was able to assign that fear to a character in the Working Dream. Once the fear was projected onto a dream-character, he could observe it without "owning" the emotion. When the Dreamer and the Critic analyzed the Working Dream, he was able to identify the character's problem. Finally he was able to recognize that the fear he had assigned to the character in his dream was actually his own. Imagery provided the mirror which allowed him to perceive a hidden facet of himself.

Through the Working Dream, you can come closer to understanding who you are and what you want and need. You won't get the answers to a lifetime of questions in one session. But you'll comprehend the process, and you can then return many times to the Dream, inviting your unconscious to reveal important information as rapidly as you are emotionally able to receive it. *Of course, this process does not substitute for psychoanalysis and should not be used alone for uncovering deeply traumatic material.*

Imagery is a powerful adjunct to other tools that help people understand their feelings—but there is no replacement for a professional therapist when serious emotional problems are involved.

ANSWERS THAT COME FROM THE INNER SELF

Ask a group of people who are in a linear mode of thinking to describe who they are and what they want. One person might say, "I'm a wife and mother; I feel good about my life but I want more quality time with my family and I wish I knew how to help my children do better at school." And another might respond, "I'm a single parent and I support three children and work as a secretary; I'm planning to make a career change because there's no way to get ahead doing what I do." And another might say, "I'm a lawyer, in a good position to move up in the firm and buy my own condo at the beach."

All of these responses may be true as far as they go, but not one of these three people answered the questions from the perspective of the inner self. While all of those answers reveal important information and are part of the fabric of the person expressing them, they don't deal with the issues we will confront in this chapter. This chapter is about the intimate part of the self. The private, complicated, exquisitely human individual who is different from every other person on earth, who has needs and longings and feelings that are separate from relationships to other people.

Your relationships with your family and your friends will be explored in the next section of this book, but in the few pages that follow, *you are the one we are trying to get to know.* The person who existed before choices were made about personal partners and children and careers is a person still. A person who has an understanding of that separateness might answer the question "Who are you? What are your needs and goals?" by saying, "I'm in transition now—sometimes confident and sometimes afraid. I'm anxious about my decisions, and no matter how confident I seem to others, sometimes I feel very much alone and out of touch with who I am and what I feel. I can't answer those questions easily, for they force me to confront how little I really know about myself."

So here, we invite the unconscious mind to help us understand not *everything* about ourselves, but *something important* about ourselves that will be of value today, in the here and now.

Who are you? Let's find an answer or two that have been tucked into hidden compartments of your unconscious. What do you need and want? You should soon have some insights that may open up a range of possibilities and, perhaps, a specific plan of action, if that's what you need at this time. You'll probably have more awareness of your inner needs after your Dreamer and your Critic have conferred at the end of the session.

You are unique in all the world. Your experiences in the Working Dream will not be the same as those of any other person who reads this book. Your imagery, in all its vividness, is as individual as your fingerprint. The story that will unfold can only be written by you.

THE TRANSITION

Remember: You need your Working Dream notebook . . . a pen . . . a quiet place. Remember the series of events that will carry you into Transition as you close your eyes and experience again: a quiet beach . . . ocean sounds . . . the colors . . . the deep relaxation . . . your personal train . . . invisible tracks moving through space and through time. (Experience the feelings through memory or by reading again pages 19–24.)

THE WORKING DREAM

Seeing Through the Pictures

You are walking through the fog that surrounds the small train station. The path is made of cobblestone or brick or perhaps some other material and you notice the texture of it and the sounds your feet make as you walk.

The path leads you to a small village and you may notice that the houses were built in earlier times. In the distance, you probably see children playing, even hear them laughing—or you might see an old man walking slowly, leaning on a gnarled cane—perhaps you see something that few people would notice. You may smell the pungent scent of a certain flower blooming nearby.

There is a most unusual bookstore in this town and you choose now to discover the wisdom that it holds for you.

As you approach the bookstore that was built so long ago, notice the color of the door. . . .

Feel the metal knob on the latch, cool against your hand.

Open the door and hear the inviting ring of a bell that announces your presence. You step inside and are aware of the smell of old books and some exotic spice that has slipped from the owner's living quarters behind the store.

There is a writing table and chair but no one is in the room. All around, from ceiling to floor, the room is lined with books bound in rich leather. There are a few whimsical touches, such as small animals made of china and some made of cloth that are scattered about as doorstops or decorations . . . or perhaps to guard the books, who can say?

Look at one animal and another, then at the others, too—with their painted faces on the china or cloth and their eyes that seem to stare right back at you.

Still you see no other person there, and you look around the room and notice that in the corner there is a narrow staircase leading upward and another that goes down into some lower rooms. And then a voice from somewhere, you may not be sure from where, says, "What you are looking for is downstairs."

Since you're not really certain what you're looking for, it might seem strange that someone else should know, but that doesn't bother you now, for in dreams you don't have to delve into the puzzlements unless you just happen to want to.

You start down the stairs, aware that a small animal (that reminds you of one of those made of china) seems to be leading the way. You hold onto the railing, feel the smooth curve of the wood . . . the stairs are rather steep and also made of wood, and the way is lit only by small candles on the walls. . . . On the sides of the stairway walls there are more books written about the past or the future, and you realize that in this place there is a gold mine of wisdom.

The steps lead further and further down, and you go deeper and deeper into the secret rooms below where you will find what you are looking for. You finally reach the bottom of the stairs and you realize that you are here to discover something you already know at some deep level of your being, but which has been hidden from you until this time.

Although the room is far below the level of the street, there is no dampness or coldness, because there is a fire burning beautifully and brightly in a small fireplace in the corner. Watch the flames and feel the warmth from the fire.

There is a chair beside the fireplace, and a small footstool. . . . Books climb the walls like colored leather vines, wandering high above you and down to the dark floor.

And the small animal that has been guiding you on your way brushes against your leg. The animal is lovable and well-meaning and has attached itself to you most fondly.

Choose a large picture-book from the shelf. Settle comfortably into the chair by the fireplace and open the book. . . . Each picture takes up a full page, so anywhere you open the book you will see two pictures, one on the right-hand page, one on the left-hand page. The pictures are rich with color and with feeling, and when you look at the pictures long enough, you realize that they are scenes from the past or the present or the future—and the images hint at secrets or memories or longings or fears.

Some pictures are as fanciful as any you might find in an elegant children's book from long ago, when the paper used in the pages was heavy and meant to last forever. The drawings are more beautiful than any you have seen anywhere except in old libraries or antiquarian bookstores . . . or in dreams.

Turn the page and observe the two pictures. One picture makes you think of a famous saying: "No one can make you feel inferior without your consent." And the other picture makes you think: "No one can make you feel successful without your consent."

You study one of the pictures and then the other. You may see a specific scene or impressions of a scene, or only abstract color swatches. Be aware of the thoughts and feelings that come to mind.

In your Working Dream notebook, write what you see or feel.

You turn the page, and one of the pictures makes you think: "Life is so brittle a thread to walk on—so easy to go wrong." On the opposite page the picture makes you think: "Life is so firm a foundation to walk on, so easy to find a footing for your dreams."

And again you choose to study one or both pictures and then make note of your insights.

You turn the page again, and this picture takes up both pages and makes you think of these phrases:

"Two men look out from the same bars; one sees mud, the other stars."

Write down what you see and what you feel.

Turn the page and let the picture evoke some thought that gives you insight into what you want or need. What do you see in the picture? Write you thoughts in your notebook.

When you are ready, close the book and place it on a nearby table or in the bookshelf.

If anything seems important to you that has not been recorded, write it in your notebook.

And now that the dream is ending, you can easily and pleasantly make the crossing to your waking reality and find that you are once again in your own workroom.

THE DREAMER AND THE CRITIC

Realize that you do not completely leave the dreamlike state when you first return—not all at once. For a little while, you are strongly influenced by the power of your unconscious and by the power of the dream. This is a good time to begin your assessment of what you learned from this experience.

If you had any difficulty seeing the pictures in your mind's eye or relating the pictures to the suggested phrases, you may want to do the exercise again; repetition increases your ability to visualize and intensifies your insights.

Did the pictures in the book provide new information for you or only affirm what you already knew to be true?

If you felt extremely positive or intensely negative about a picture or your association to it, you can be sure that some sensitive area was touched upon by the suggestion. Be aware that this reaction provides a fertile field that can yield greater understanding if you are prepared to work with those feelings. What scenes held the greatest fascination for you?

Begin to write your associations to what you experienced. Then go back and circle all the ideas or insights that seem most important for you to remember.

Think back—when you studied the pictures in the book, what did they reveal to you about your self-image and your longings and your fears? Were you attracted to the negative or the positive suggestions? Did any of the pictures surprise you by their content or by the emotions they invoked? Did you choose pictures that held insights into your deepest longings and needs—or did you choose pictures that were more superficial in content, thereby avoiding confrontation with those sensitive feelings?

Remember that you can always go back again and go deeper, if you choose. You can change the "suggestions" and you can change the pictures. You can choose to see all that you are ready to see. I am your guide for the journey, but you are the one who selects the content of your Dream. Be patient with your Dream Maker; important revelations happen in their own good time and The Dream Maker gives you only what you are prepared to receive.

Consider how this game—which is part dream, part play, part work—can help you alter your perceptions, or can indicate actions you might take to make your life more fulfilling. Remember that you shouldn't act on any of the feelings that have emerged from your unconscious mind until you review these feelings again—at a later time when the analytical Critic of your left brain is in greater control. For now, when your Critic has evaluated your feelings, write down your insights about them and about the possibilities for actions. Reread them a little later to determine what action you feel you should take; you may then find it helpful to refer to your notes.

Personal Stories

Helen Pankowsky, M.D., who was mentioned briefly in Chapter 2, is a psychiatrist who has recently moved to Los Angeles. She seems to have a naturally playful spirit and delights in the surprises she discovers in Working Dreams. Single and in her early thirties, she is now taking additional training in child psychiatry at the UCLA/Harbor Medical Center; it was for this training that she left Texas and came to California.

If you recall, in Chapter 2 Helen chose a seat in the train that only allowed her to look backward—until she recognized the metaphor and acknowledged that she had a choice about whether to look forward or backward in her life.

This time, when she experienced the Transition, Helen wrote about it in far different terms. Beginning with her images on the beach, she wrote:

I'm aware that there is glitter interspersed in the air. Sparking, iridescent, luminescent flecks in my space. The glitter settles and becomes the sand. I relax on this beautiful beach until my train arrives.

My compartment resembles a glass-enclosed solarium on top of the train with plants and a single chair. My seat is soft and plush. I can look in any direction that I choose . . . glass is everywhere.

Further metaphors for her feelings about moving to Los Angeles emerged from the suggestion, "Life is so firm a foundation, so easy to find a footing for your dreams." She felt as if she was looking down at a footprint in the dirt. Her foot fit there; it was her path—but she couldn't see the whole picture, only one step at a time.

For "Two men look out from the same bars, one sees mud, the other stars," she saw a man staring at the mud:

. . . the bars that imprison him become darker, thicker, stronger. The mud covers him and consumes him. The other man gazes at the stars. He sees their beauty and the more he does, the less the bars contain him. They begin to fade and then melt away. He reaches for a star, holds it in his hand. Then he soars and flies among the stars finally becoming one with them.

"Glitter" was a word that occurred several times as Helen reported her experiences in the Transition and in the Working Dream. Because relocation in Los Angeles is such a recurrent theme for her, I thought she might have had an association to the negative, superficial image of "glitter" which makes some people think of our luminous city as "Tinsel Town." But Helen thought of the glitter as something magical and wonderful, a metaphor for exciting opportunities that are all around her.

In the suggestion, "No one can make you feel successful without your consent," Helen imagined that the glitter represented all the opportunities available to her. She tried to pick up a piece of the glitter to examine it more closely, saying that it seemed as if each sparkling piece was like one second in every minute, in every hour, in every year, full of potential. She couldn't make out the pictures that she imagined were within the sparkles, but she didn't doubt that they were there, if only she could discern them.

She was also aware that a black liquid was starting to form on the upper *right-hand* corner of the picture (which many psychiatrists believe corresponds to the destructive judgmental aspects of the personality which are centered in the *left* hemisphere of the brain). She recognized it as a negative, destructive quality and demanded, in her notebook, that it get out of her dream. It reminded her that she has the power to control the destructive aspects of an inner critic who acts out too strongly. The dream helped her reaffirm her power over her responses.

Barbara Sax, M.D., had a reaction to this Working Dream that was quite different from her experiences in the forest; she said she imagined one star was laughing—and she played with the implications that more laughter was a very good thing in one's life, and that she could choose to have more in hers.

Her last picture, in which no phrase was suggested, was abstract in design but made Barbara realize that she needs to take time for some things she wants to do for herself, things that she has pushed aside these last few years. She decided that she must open one of those doors she has kept locked for so long; beyond the door she imagined time for herself—time to write poetry, time to dream her own dreams. She also recognized that if the door was to remain unlocked she would have to take her Dream Maker's message to heart. Wanting a time apart was not enough; she would have to make specific plans to be alone—and then be as responsible about caring for her own needs as she is about caring for others.

Mary Christianson, M.D., a child psychiatrist, also realized that she needs to have more time to herself, but with her heavy schedule it isn't easy to arrange. Mary gets tremendous satisfaction from her work, but when you spend your days with hurting and sometimes abused children, you need to find ways to keep balance in your life. I've known Mary for more than twenty years, always treasured her friendship and admired the way she approaches problems from a matter-of-fact, how-are-we-going-to-fix-it point of view. She is married to a psychiatrist and they have two grown sons.

Mary assigned herself the role of "Doubting Thomas" in our group. She said she came to test the exercises out of curiosity—to see how others responded; she didn't really expect to gain much for herself—but she thought it would be an interesting experience. The first two sessions she moved slowly, keeping distance between herself and the Dreams.

In the suggestion, "Life is so firm a foundation, so easy to form a footing for your dreams," she had a fanciful image of playfulness and returned to the image of the beach, where laughing children reminded her to take more time to nurture her own inner child. It was an easy Dream that she created for herself this day, with no new information. Later, Mary's approach changed, as you will see.

Recycling the Dream

Your experiences in the Working Dream can help you understand yourself and your needs more clearly. You can recreate the dream as many times as it pleases you to do so, and each time your experiences will reveal different insights. Many people discover that they go much deeper into the experience the second time or the third. Dreams that hint of secrets never told often reveal their mysteries when you return to them with a receptive mind.

CHAPTER 5

MAKING PEACE WITH THE PAST

—————◆—————

From the rubble of old clichés, some tattered phrases are occasionally worth recalling—if for no greater purpose than to help us explore the popular conceptions we choose to accept or reject. You can't turn back the clock, they say, or hold onto the past. Well, personally speaking, it isn't that I hold onto the past—the problem is, the past holds onto me.

The problem isn't mine alone; few people would claim that lingering grievances haven't occasionally weighted them down and prevented them from moving on. I remember some notes I made about that in my journal years ago:

> Having acquired over the years some cumbersome things, I decided before moving on, to throw them away. Small pity: a sack of grievances I collected one summer in New York City, a box of questions from a winter in Paris, a stack of illusions now obsolete, a vial of tears from a lonely street; this and more—stored like potatoes near the door of my past. I moved on. Behind me, the old discarded things, abandoned with the trash. But not a week had passed when, while looking through a closet (already cluttered), I discovered a strange and disturbing thing. For there among tomorrow's plans lay a sack of grievances, a box of questions, a stack of illusions. . . .

We can't discard any portion of our past—or the memories that reach with their long tentacles into the present. We can, however, perceive them differently. In this chapter I'll suggest an exercise that can break their hold on our emotions.

Willa Cather wrote, "There are only two or three human stories, and they go on repeating themselves as fiercely as if they had never happened before." It's my bet that one of these universal stories has to do with the lingering of old memories and feelings, and the power they claim in the present and the long shadow they cast into the future.

This chapter is dedicated to all of us who struggle with lingering grievances that neither time nor good intentions have overcome. The experience you'll have in the Working Dream will not replace the value of psychotherapy for helping you recover from excessive wounding of the spirit, but it will provide an adjunct to other survival skills and can give you needed release. If the resentful feelings return, as they do on occasion, you can return to the Working Dream and cast them out again. Some people find that the grievances stay away for longer and then even longer periods at a time; I hope this will prove true for you.

FORGIVENESS

The power of forgiveness to heal painful memories is legendary. If real forgiveness occurs, your perception is altered forever. This is, of course, the best of all options. But if you have not yet reached the spiritual level where you are able to forgive atrocious deeds, then the Working Dream will provide exercises to help you for the present time. In a higher consciousness, one can forgive others, forgive circumstances—even forgive oneself; until that time, grievances can be dealt with in more earthly terms.

FROM THE BEGINNING

Adults sometimes try to pretend that childhood is a place you leave behind when you grow wise—or up. A place that you abandon, shed like skin, when you come of age. People who are knowledgeable about matters of the heart (more accurately the brain and psyche) claim otherwise. There was never a thing you deeply feared or wanted that had no seed, no root, or starting, in childhood's fertile soil.

THE OLDEST OF FRIENDS

In *The Right-Brain Experience*, I interviewed a number of creative thinkers who were very much in touch with the realization that the inner child and the inner adult coexist; anything we can do to keep them aware of each other's needs and feelings is worth the effort. The creator of the "Peanuts" cartoons, Charles Schulz, keeps a wooden horse from his boyhood very near his drawing board. Writer Ray Bradbury has an office cluttered with childhood memorabilia. Engineering professor Robert McKim keeps his old familiar teddy bear in his office at Stanford University (which, it seems to me, takes a bit of courage).

Recently I was reading a book of poems by the scientist Loren Eiseley, who held a distinguished chair in anthropology at the University of Pennsylvania before his death in 1977. In *Notes of an Alchemist*, he wrote about the value of a special childhood treasure in a way that transcends sentimentality:

THE FACE OF THE LION*

The moth-eaten lion with shoe-button eyes
is lumpy by modern standards
    and his mane
scarcely restorable.
    I held him in my arms
    when I was small.
I held him when my parents quarreled
as they did often while
    I shrank away.
    My beast has come

---

* Charles Scribner's Sons, 1972. Used by permission of the publisher.

down the long traverse of such years and travel
        as have left outworn or lost
beds slept in, women loved, hall clocks that struck
        wrong hours,
. . . but the lion
sits on the shelf above my desk
       and I,
          near-sighted now,
take comfort that he looks
    forthright and bold
        as when
my hands were small,
     as when
my brain received him living,
      something kind
      where little kindness was.

The mirror tells me that my hair is grey
but the wild animist within my heart
refuses to acknowledge him a toy
. . . no, the lion lives
      and watches me
as I do him.
    Should I forget
the hours in the blizzard dark,
      the tears
spilled silent while I clutched his mane?
He is very quiet there upon the shelf,
as I am here, but we were silent
      even then,
past words,
    past time.
    We waited for the light
and fell asleep when no light ever came.

No matter how acclaimed the scientist or successful the businessperson, tucked at the nucleus of every being is the child who calls out in dreams, longing to be heard.

Through the metaphors of dreams come the realities of our feelings and our needs. If we can translate these messages into life, they have served us well.

THE TRANSITION

Remember: You need your Working Dream notebook . . . a pen . . . a quiet place. Remember the series of events that will carry you into Transition as you close your eyes and experience again: a quiet beach . . . ocean sounds . . . the colors . . . the deep relaxation . . . your personal train . . . invisible tracks moving through space and through time. (Experience the feelings through memory or by reading again pages 19–24.)

THE WORKING DREAM

Scenes from a Distant Past

Your special train has carried you backward in time to childhood where both good things and bad things happened to everyone, though we tend to forget that sometimes. You know that every life is affected by good and evil and also by well-meaning people who made unwise choices. Still, we have all chosen which memories to nurture in our adult lives.

You have arrived, not to the place of your childhood but to a place of fantasy where you have greater control than you had when you were a child. In this experience you will have great power if you choose to exercise it and the choice, as always, is your own.

Take the path that leads through the field and know that the path is right for you to take, and you intuitively know that this is the way you should go on this day. The field is a profusion of color, for it is springtime. The surrounding hills are gently rolling and the field is inviting and so enticing in its simple, natural beauty that you lie down to rest.

Feel the grass beneath you, lush as a clover bed, feel the air, warm against your skin. There is the smell of some wild and wonderful thing growing nearby. In your dream you notice how blue the sky appears and how white the clouds. Notice how you can control the shape of the clouds by your thoughts. Cumulus and downy against the blue sky, they respond to your thoughts, changing form with any whim of your imagination.

Watch the clouds and play with the fantasies as you did so many years ago.

There is a gentle animal nearby. . . . You are curious about this animal, which may be a rabbit or perhaps a tame and kind-hearted tiger or even a small giraffe that is no larger in size than a rabbit or a squirrel, and it may be small enough to fit in the palm of your hand, if you wish. . . . Let the animal come close enough so that you can get a clear image of how it looks at this moment. You might even pet it, if you have a mind to, for this animal is pure in spirit and is willing to be your friend.

Your animal scampers in front of you and, like a child, you follow. There is a clear trail leading out of the meadow, and you may be surprised to see that suddenly there is a drop in terrain, and your animal scoots down, down further to a lower plot of ground and you follow.

At this lower level, suddenly the grass changes color and is not green at all, but lavender . . . and this strange grass spreads across this childhood place, and still you follow this small creature to deeper levels into a world so magical and mysterious and wondrous that the sheer beauty of it invites you to proceed.

And there is a cave that is safe and beautiful, that is filled with stalactites and stalagmites that have grown there for millions of years. The color of them is so exquisite that it fairly takes your breath away and still your animal leads you into greater depths and finally scoots through a small hole which you are much too large to enter. Only a very young child could fit through that hole, and you can only lie on the ground of the cave and look through the hole to the wondrous playroom on the other side and wish that you could enter too.

"You will have to be very small to come in," your animal says, and you agree. "So think yourself small and it will be done—come on, I want your company," the small creature beckons.

And so you scrunch your body down as small as it will go and close your eyes and imagine that as you crawl through that hole you will become a child again. You are able to do this through the power of your imagination and you can clearly see that this is a whimsical place, designed for people with a sense of humor (or at least a sense of metaphor) who realize that things are not always as they seem.

In this room, which is like none you were ever in before, are rows of shelves, and you see some animals made of cloth and others of fur; you see trucks and houses, clowns and dolls, and a puppet stage with several puppets and even a box with something inside.

Look again, and discover that some of the things in this room are very old; in fact, everything in that room has been used and loved and dropped and comforted and thrown about by careless hands and picked up by loving hands and every toy has been pushed by children who did not care and played with by children who cared deeply.

And you realize that, in one way, the lives of people are not too dissimilar from the lives of toys. For no one—and few toys—live in a truly protected place, and a place that could keep a person safe would also be a cage that would keep a person innocent of life and, when you think about it, that is not such a good idea at all.

Wisdom comes from the most unexpected sources and from the most unexpected places and you can learn from almost anything, if you try.

If you look around, you can see a rabbit made of velveteen, and another that stole cabbages from a Scotsman's farm, and a prince from a kingdom on a distant star. There are other animals who did battle against the odds and sometimes won. You can see clowns whose smiles are painted over tear-stained cheeks and a horse that rode against the storm. They survived it all.

And on those shelves are some animals that belonged to you many years ago, and if they could talk they would tell tales of your laughter and your tears and your loneliness and your wonder, and of childhood's magic and fear. And you realize that some children who seemed to have life easy had it hard in secret ways, and some who had it harder than you can imagine have survived in spite of that, though surely there are scars, if one could see beneath the surface of courage and strength.

Choose an animal (or a doll) from the shelf that belongs to your childhood and hold it to you as you make a decision that is yours alone to make. You can hold this small comforting creature, as you did long ago, and without even naming the names of the sorrows, you can imagine that your old sorrows pour from the eyes of the creature in your arms and from the eyes of the animals and dolls on the shelf and the tears form a stream that rolls down to the corner of the far wall. . . .

The tears are transformed into a heavy mass of black pain that is large enough to contain all the tears that have been spent in sorrow. . . . Now it solidifies into the shape that you see before you.

And now from your own heart pour the confessions, not by name but by feeling, and you imagine that all the hurtful choices you made and all the grievances you have held in your mind pour forth and are absorbed by the mass of pain across the room.

And if there are more recent grievances that you want to release, let go of them now . . . let them flow into the dark mass of pain across the room.

And the mass expands with the weight of your sadness and anger and all the resentments that you have nurtured throughout your lifetime.

Imagine that the floor in that far corner of the room opens wide, and the mass, huge and black and heavy as iron, falls into that hole and drops down through a shaft into the depths of the earth. It falls deeper and deeper and continues falling until it reaches the core of the earth and is consumed by the heat of the molten lava that exists in the center of the world.

It is finished now, these tears, for they have rolled out of your life and they have been transformed. Look at the animals and the dolls, and see that their faces are dry and their eyes are twinkling again and there are smiles on their faces, not because there was no pain, but because they chose to release the pain. They lived through the reality and survived. They lived through the memory and survived. If you have survived the reality, you can survive the memory of it, too.

And at this moment you feel cleansed of all that you have chosen to harbor in your mind that is harmful and you feel refreshed, and there is a spirit of love that fills the room and a spirit of goodness that envelops you, and you determine that from this point on you will choose which memories you will nurture.

In your Working Dream notebook, write down your experiences in this dream. Record what you saw and what you felt.

And in this childhood room there is a puppet stage, and on the stage are puppets that remind you of people you have known or know now, people who have made you weep or made you rage against the night sky in dreams, or made you hate them or hate yourself. You need not name these people now; only know that they exist on this puppet stage.

And all of the puppets, you realize now, have problems of their own, for they have not mastered their own choices or made the choices that were kind.

But if you are able to forgive the people who have hurt you, do it now.

And if you are able to forgive circumstance (or fate or God) for the events over which you had no control, do it now.

And if you can forgive yourself for the hurtfulness that you have caused to yourself and to others, do it now.

And if you have the desire to be forgiven by another, seek that forgiveness now.

If you can let go of anything that keeps you from experiencing the highest form of love, do it now.

If you can do these things, you will feel the most exquisite pleasure . . . a sensation of lightness . . . a spirit of joy that transcends any feelings you have ever known . . . and you will feel the joy that passes all understanding.

An ancient wise man once said: "There is nothing I can give you which you do not already have. But there is much that, while I cannot give it, you can take. Take Peace. . . ."

Give Peace to yourself as a present. If you choose to give Peace to yourself, you have begun to fill the void that was left by grievances. And you can continue to fill that void with other positive feelings, such as love (for yourself and others), kindness (to yourself and others), and hope (for yourself and for others too).

Choose Peace.

Choose Love.

Choose Hope.

In your notebook, write down what you have experienced and what you have learned.

And now the dream begins to end, and you pass through time and space and return, gently and easily, to your workroom, and when you are ready, open your eyes.

THE DREAMER AND THE CRITIC

If you were able to feel release from the grievances, ask yourself these questions (and write the answers in your notebook).

Do you feel lighter without the burden of resentment?

Do you hope the peaceful feelings will last?

Do you believe you have the power to reduce your receptiveness to negative feelings in the future?

Your Critic may point out that resentments have a way of crawling back into your psyche in the quiet hours of the night . . . or when some event triggers the memory of the pain. And your Critic may suggest that you could return to this Dream many times, or devise a dream of your own that is directly related to your situation. Over and over again, destructive thoughts try to intrude upon your spirit of Peace. Choose Peace again . . . and again.

If you were able to feel release from the pain, but could not bring yourself to forgive those who have hurt you, consider these questions:

Is there any way in which you benefit from feeling the resentment?

Do you want to hold onto the resentment for some reason that you may not understand?

If you cannot (or don't choose to) release the anger, would you consider burying it somewhere out of sight so that it doesn't keep you from experiencing more positive feelings?

Now make the choice that is best for you to make. . . . And let the power of goodness fill the void . . . and choose your perceptions wisely from this point forward.

Personal Stories

Several interesting stories have emerged from groups participating in this exercise but perhaps the most instructive are the cases in which the exercise was *not* successfully completed.

A lawyer from New York refused to experience a Working Dream on the subject of forgiving grievances for a very interesting reason: He said he felt so angry at someone who was making his life miserable that he wasn't ready to let go of his anger. He recognized that he could choose peace through forgiveness, but he just wasn't ready to allow his rage to diminish. Usually this man is quick to forgive and he claims that old grievances from his childhood were long ago put to rest. His present situation was quite another matter—his rage was intense and he felt the power of his emotion strangely satisfying and he wasn't about to give it up.

The only value of the exercise to this man was that he saw, quite clearly, the depth of his feelings and his attachment to those feelings. He had a choice and he chose anger—but at least he acknowledged that he had the power to determine his response; he claimed responsibility for nurturing his resentment and said that he would give it up at a later time. At the present, the taste of rage was just too sweet.

There was a woman in Connecticut who had trouble with this particular Working Dream. (She experienced the Dream in a group situation but reported to me in private.) She was not accustomed to recognizing feelings of intense resentment within herself; strict religious training had ensured that she would repress any conscious awareness of prolonged anger.

At the time of this private session, Ann had just discovered that her husband was involved in a business deal with people who threatened her greatly. She didn't approve of their business ethics, certainly didn't trust them, and she believed that her husband's "handshake deals" put her in jeopardy. At one level, she wanted to confront her husband with all that she had found out about his secret dealings, but for the fifteen years of their marriage she had never been able to confront him directly with any kind of criticism. When she had tried, he was quickly angered and retaliated with threats that were devastating.

Now that she was preparing herself psychologically to confront him, she was reluctant to submit herself to an exercise in forgiveness. She thought she needed her anger as a catalyst for action. Old psychological patterns pulled strongly against her decision, as she was tempted to "turn loose" of her anger and return to her passive behavior.

Believing that she needed her anger, it's no wonder that she was reluctant to encounter a Working Dream to achieve forgiveness. Whether or not one believes that anger is a positive attitude in her case, it is her anger, and her right to decide whether to keep it. (Two months later, she still had not confronted her husband—neither had she released her anger and fear about the situation. Clearly, other choices would have been wiser.)

Mary Christianson, M.D., psychiatrist, had perceived her mother as a woman who was resentful of the demands of mothering seven children. During the Dream, she became aware of how her mother was psychologically ill-prepared for such a large family. If her mother did not provide the kind of mothering Mary needed and wanted, she did provide all that she was able to give. "She was a brilliant woman who gave up her own talents—her own uniqueness—to try to fit into the stereotypical role of what a woman should be at that time." Mary said. "She would have fit easily into the 1980's but was out of place in the 20's and 30's. She loved to sing, to paint, to read books, to attend lectures—but instead, she had children."

Mary said that the full awareness of her mother's situation—and her ability to understand her mother—did not become evident to her during years of analysis, but in fact, began to emerge in a previous Dream and then appeared vividly and powerfully as a result of this one.

Mary's insights did not evolve directly from the actual script itself, but were the result of the cumulative effect of several exercises and Mary's ability to take the Dream in directions that were appropriate for her.

And so it is with Dreams. They are not linear, and what I suggest may not always be what you experience. As often as not, your Working Dream may lead you into other discoveries. For Dreams will not always play our games on our own terms and sometimes they will use any setting to stage their own performances and express the deepest needs of the Dreamer. Dream Makers usually know what they are doing and how much we are ready to accept. And even when the gift we receive isn't the gift we asked for, it is usually a pretty good fit.

Your Own Decisions

Ask anyone who has ever truly forgiven another for a major grievance and you'll realize how freeing the experience can be. Consider your own life, and decide if there is someone you need to forgive—for your own sake, if not for theirs. You may find that when you relinquish your resentment, the space it filled in your life is then able to contain an abundance of good feelings—about yourself and about others, too.

CHAPTER 6

LIVING
THE QUESTIONS

———◆———

"Be patient toward all that is unsolved in your heart; learn to live the questions themselves," Rainer Maria Rilke advised a young poet, years ago. That's hard for most of us to do. We have such a need to believe we're on the right road that we often choose the most obvious path instead of the better one. Many a fine opportunity has been lost because a person was unprepared to "live the questions" for a while.

Much has been said about procrastination as a major problem of many people, but not much is mentioned about the value of waiting for the intuitive self to tell you when to press on. Procrastination is not the same thing as living the questions, though an observer might not be able to tell which mode of thinking was in process. We need to distinguish a neurotic inability to make minor decisions (What will I order for dinner? What will I wear to the party?) from procrastinations that are based on inner wisdom. Sometimes we know intuitively that we should wait for new information or for a more appropriate time.

Suspending judgment (or action) is often a way of responding to the wisdom of the unconscious. We just need to be honest with ourselves about whether our inability to act is based upon unrealistic fears, or whether it is based on prudent restraint.

THE INDECISIVE MIND

Why is it so difficult for people to defer judgment? What emotions arise from indecisiveness, and how can we take charge of our responses? There is a fear of powerlessness in indecision—a feeling of impotence. We are vulnerable, standing in the waiting room of a difficult situation, hoping that a clear sense of direction will swing open the doors and let us get on with our lives.

But sometimes waiting itself is a wise and courageous decision. It provides a time apart. As you live the questions, you can look inward and discover your own specialness. Learn to be receptive to the longings that reveal themselves in the stillness. Be ready for wonderful surprises and be prepared to accept them when they come. Also be prepared to create good situations for yourself for there's no guarantee that circumstance will place them in your path.

Keep in mind, though, that while it is one person's wisdom to wait, it is another's to act. You are the only one who can know what is right for you. Don't be too quick to label yourself a procrastinator; first, take a hard look at your motives for waiting.

In January of 1985 I was in Sweden meeting with a client, Gunnar Wessman, Chairman of the Board of Pharmacia, an international pharmaceutical corporation. In Stockholm it was 29 degrees below zero and in nearby Uppsala, where we were, it was only slightly colder. Our work for the day was finished: We could feel the cold seeping through the double panes of glass at the restaurant where we sat with aperitifs, continuing to discuss the themes that had brought a thin-blooded Californian so close to the North Pole this winter evening.

Gaining Control

Our thoughts kept returning to the work, and Gunnar Wessman, who makes decisions that affect many people in his multimillion-dollar corporation, offered a helpful comment about the philosophy of the waiting process:

> Instead of saying I am indecisive, let us say I have decided not to decide. That perspective gives us a sense of power over the situation; our lives seem once again in our control.

You should actually wait as long as possible to make a decision, because if there are five possibilities, as soon as you make a
decision, the four other choices are gone.

Psychologists have a phrase for the act of making a decision
before it has had time to ripen in the mind; they call it "premature
closure." Many a fine idea has never been given the time or the
climate to emerge from the unconscious mind into consciousness.

In a television commercial Orson Welles said, "We never sell a
wine before its time." That same concept should be applied to all
of our important areas of decision-making. We should be certain
that our plans have matured before we send them out into the
world.

To Play the Waiting Game

When we are afraid to act, sometimes the reason is based on well-
founded insights that are clearly evident in our unconscious
minds. Sometimes, however, we don't take appropriate actions
because of fears that cling to our confidence like barnacles to a
ship, and we need to clean them off before we are free to move on.
On occasion, the barnacles resist our efforts to disengage them
and we must just learn how to go on in spite of them. Jean Rostand
said, "Real work lies in knowing how to wait." True enough, but I
would rephrase that to read, "Real work lies in knowing *when* to
wait." We need to know how to gain access to the insights in our
unconscious minds so that we can evaluate properly whether we
are procrastinating, or living the questions. One is weakness, the
other power.

Things that Go Bump in the Night

Children are not the only ones to wake at night with fears of wild
beasts and monsters; it's just that children externalize their anxieties, projecting them onto "the other," and mature adults recognize them for what they are—symbols of inner conflicts. Real
maturity comes in recognizing that everyone has his or her own
haunting creatures that wander through the darkest dreams and in
the twilight sleep of dawn; it's important to keep them in perspective and not to give them greater power than they deserve.

There's an old Zen saying that's making the rounds on the West Coast, as of this writing: "Sit, walk, or run, but don't wobble." Living the questions is a way of sitting quietly in readiness; procrastination is the worst kind of wobbling.

The exercises in this chapter will help you to name your fears and assess the wisdom (or foolishness) of delaying a specific action. Choose wisely from the suggestions your unconscious brings forth in this Working Dream.

THE TRANSITION

Remember: You need your Working Dream notebook . . . a pen . . . a quiet place. Remember the series of events that will carry you into Transition as you close your eyes and experience again: a quiet beach . . . ocean sounds . . . the colors . . . the deep relaxation . . . your personal train . . . invisible tracks moving through space and through time. (Experience the feelings through memory or by reading again pages 19–24.)

THE WORKING DREAM

Stalking the Gold Ring

The path from the train station leads to a road that will take you to a carnival that has pitched its tents on the outskirts of a small town.

> It is night when you arrive on the midway and you watch the games being played and the booths on either side of you are crowded with people throwing balls, tossing beanbags . . .
> There's the clown and the tattooed lady . . .
> And the dancers from far-off lands.

The ferris wheel is a circle of light against the night sky; its one empty seat is a ladle that catches stars.

> The merry-go-round draws you by the sound of its music, the tinny song of carnivals and dreams of carnivals, and you let the music tug on your attention, pulling you in.

There's a ticket in your hand, so you can get on the merry-go-round any time you choose . . . you can select any horse to ride, any one at all. . . . Feel the breadth of its back and the aura of fantasy that surrounds it.

Now it starts, the slow circling, the up and down action of the horse and the turning action of the carousel. Feel the wood beneath you as you did when you were a child, or wished to do when you were a child.

Above you hang the rings, waiting to be grabbed from their place above you as you pass. You watch them, noticing the colors . . . the red and purple . . . the yellow and green . . . blue now and amber—and one, only one, is gold.

Go around once . . . and again . . .

Catch the gold ring.

You are the winner of the gold ring and the attendant gives you the prize. It is a paper with something written on it that you will want to read, for it has to do with an important decision you will make. Open the paper and discover that some valuable advice has been given to you, advice about the decision you have wanted to make and have resisted making. The paper may tell you to wait for more information, or it may tell you it is time to confront your procrastinations.

If you can't read the words on the page, imagine what they say.

If the answer doesn't come to you, perhaps there is a reason that you are not yet prepared to see the solution. Be patient with yourself and turn your attention toward the sounds you hear. . . .

Music, soft and rhythmical, comes from the midway. Follow the sound of the music which hints of the Caribbean or of Mardi Gras or of gypsies.

There is a parade coming down the midway and the music is part of the parade and the sound washes over you. . . . Feel it touching your skin and breathe it in to your lungs and let the sound wrap itself around you, making you part of the celebration.

There is a lumbering elephant with the sequined lady riding high . . . her eyes smile at you through slits in her makeup.

Dancers pass you wearing masks . . .

There is a clown.

Now the cast of characters changes, becoming a parade of people you know or once knew . . . memories are gathered from one time and pressed up against another.

Watch them as they pass, these people who were (and are) significant in your life. Hold the memories to you and let them go. . . . You can always come back, you can always return to the parade, for it belongs to you and is always available to you, ready to entertain and instruct you.

Now think of a decision you want to make.

Notice that the parade includes people who have insights into your needs and into the wisdom that you need for this decision.

Let one of them approach you. Ask any question you want to ask and listen for the answers as the soft music continues around you, swirling around the crowd, holding you to the Dream.

Now someone who is exquisitely wise and who will give you the finest advice possible for your situation appears in the parade. Perhaps this is someone you have known or even someone who lived long ago, or perhaps this is a fortune-teller who can read dreams and see into the future.

Ask that person whether the time is right for you to make the important decision you have wanted to make.

Ask if you should be patient, waiting for new information. If the advice is that you should live the question, then ask what you should do in preparation for the time of decision-making. If you are to wait, it is important to understand why you are waiting, and to be aware of small signs that will direct your course.

Stay in the dream as long as the insights are coming, as long as you feel comfortable there, and it is nourishing for you to be in the parade.

When you are ready to come back to the here and now, bring yourself back to your workroom and open your eyes, but retain the mood of the dream so that you can take your Dream notebook and record what you experienced in the Dream. Remember. . . .

The midway . . . the carousel . . . the horse . . . the golden ring . . . the message . . . the parade . . . the characters in the parade . . . your questions . . . and the answers . . . and your insights.

THE DREAMER AND THE CRITIC

To combine the skills of both hemispheres, you'll need to assess the insights that came to you during this Dream. In your notebook, take a double-page spread and fill the space with a dozen or more circles. Think of them as balloons that cover the pages. You can use these to cluster ideas, which is much more effective than making lists for dealing with creative ideas. In each circle, put a few words that remind you of some awareness that came to you as a result of the exercise. This may be a new insight, or it may be an old awareness, but if it was an important part of the Dream, make note of it in the circles. Some of these insights will seem valuable and others will not. It doesn't matter how many ideas there are that you *don't* choose to act on, what matters are the ones that are valuable, that you choose to keep and use.

Professional photographers working on large advertising accounts or journalistic assignments might take hundreds of photographs to get the one that is superior to all the rest. When a photographer wins an award for the picture, it doesn't matter how many were thrown away. The same is true of writers, who often have a wastebasket full of crumpled pieces of paper. No one asks them about the stories that never came to life—they only judge the ones that made it through the competition to the printed page.

These images can be helpful, for in matters of life's important decisions, shouldn't we have as many options to choose from as we possibly can? And isn't it all right to have a garbage can full of unusable ideas, if just one gem has been discovered?

As you test the value of each of your ideas, place them against this yardstick: What are the logical reasons to wait before you move? What are the emotional reasons to wait before you move? What do you have to lose by waiting? What do you have to gain?

It is important to point out, from time to time, that these Dreams are only the way in which your unconscious mind communicates with your consciousness. Nothing magical is happening here: You are merely gaining access to the valuable insights of your Inner Advisor.

Personal Stories

Jay Myers, the psychobiologist who imagined the fence made of match-sticks in Chapter 3, had a moving experience in a carnival Dream. He was deeply relaxed in the Transition, and instead of taking his personal train, he flew above the tracks to the small town where the carnival tents were pitched. (As I have reported in earlier works, dreams of flying are experienced by an astonishing percentage of highly creative people. People who know how to experience a flying dream are also able to reach a state of deep relaxation rather quickly.)

On the way from the beach to the carnival, Jay took his personal flight over the jungles of Peru and saw an ancient Mayan city which he would like to return to in another Dream.

When Jay got on the carousel, the horse seemed real, yet it was constrained. Although it was alive, the horse never tried to escape the well-ordered pattern of its circular journey. Jay caught the golden ring, yet the message on the paper was unclear; he moved on to the midway and the parade.

The parade was vivid, alive with characters that he described in explicit detail: the elephant, and then the camel . . . and then suddenly his father became part of the parade. Jay's father had died six months before. His presence seemed to fill the dream, and when Jay talked about the experience moments later, he was visibly moved. His father had been fascinated by camels, had collected stories about them, and Jay had always meant to find some obscure piece of literature that would be a special gift.

The advice Jay received from his father was not directly given, but was communicated clearly when his father said, "Jay, I was never afraid to move around from place to place." And there were also words of affirmation, as his father expressed his pride and his affection.

Since one of Jay's ongoing themes has to do with his career choice (research in artificial intelligence fascinates him as much as brain research), his father's declaration was not so much advice as it was a statement of attitude. Jay took it as reassurance that it might not be a bad idea to explore other options.

Suddenly he realized what was written on the paper from the golden ring: "All paths have value," he said, recalling without doubt or hesitation what he had chosen not to see before his father entered his Dream. Jay would have preferred a less ambiguous answer—but the ones he received, from his father and from the prize for the golden ring, affirmed his need for further exploration. He needs to live the questions for awhile.

At the carnival, Mary Christianson, M.D., psychiatrist, became a child again in a small Texas town, walking the midway with her father as she did long ago.

It was the carnival barker who had attracted her in the past— he called to her now, in the Dream: She could see the colors and the textures and hear the carnival sounds once more. There was a sense of adventure, of mystery, but her father pulled her away, warning her . . . of what? She didn't know.

Mary's thoughts flashed to another moment from her childhood . . . there was a banana boat on the river . . . a man, the ship's captain . . . he told her stories of the sea . . . of distant ports. . . . How old was she then, she wondered? Nine maybe, or ten. Her mother warned her not to go to the dock and not to talk to the captain. The captain had offered her a ride on his boat and she had wanted to go with him, she recalled, but instead had run home.

Mary is aware that she has often pulled back from adventurous choices, playing life safe. Now she seems ready to explore new possibilities.

"I know what I'm going to do," she said to the group. "I'm going to buy a house . . . somewhere by a river . . . a place to get away . . . Northern California maybe. Nothing big, just a small place. But something that's mine." And then the practical Mary I have known for such a long time declared, "I could rent it out so it would really be a business investment, but I would know it was there when I wanted it."

She's determined to act on the feeling, to start looking for that small house on a river that represents delicious choices left untaken, and a place to dream her own uninterrupted dreams.

I'm always quick to recommend that people not move too fast on suggestions from their right-brain, spontaneous self. Ideas that seem "out of character" need to be carefully evaluated.

Suddenly Mary started talking about changing the way she dresses, which, though stylish and elegant, is always tailored and conservative to the proverbial "T." Mary's perception of herself is changing; it seems that she has lived the questions long enough.

CHAPTER 7

DISCOVERING YOUR PERSONAL STYLE

———◆———

Personal style is a presentation of your specialness. It makes a statement about your attitude toward life, how you feel about yourself and others. Personal style is the manifestation of who you are—expressed in aesthetic, tactile, metaphoric ways.

Personal style has little to do with the current rage in the fashion world or how others may think you should look. Slender ladies in Paris couturier gowns or men wearing the latest Italian designer suits have a distinctive flair, but that's not the sort of style I'm referring to. Personal style is hard to define, but you'll know it when you see it every time.

Einstein had style. That mane of wild hair that claimed its own freedom sprang from the head of a man for whom freedom was a passion and a cause. John Kennedy had style and it also reflected his inner persona; it just wouldn't have been the same if he had worn polyester suits and Hawaiian shirts. Lauren Bacall has style—and so does Mary Lou Retton.

Style is not only what you wear, but the sound of your voice and the kind of living quarters you choose and the look of the dog who owns you. Style is the way you move. It is the way you call a friend on a rainy Sunday and suggest something spontaneous, something outrageous, or something quaint—depending upon your own personal style.

I know a woman who wears second-hand clothes and lives in a converted loft that's full of antique hobbyhorses and handcrafted masks. There are textures of stained glass and heavy wooden beams; there's chamber music and abstract art and conversation that weaves in and out of cultures and philosophies. Once you've met her you don't forget her—that's style.

There are those who think that personal style is of merely superficial significance, and that it doesn't matter how you dress or where you live or whether your haircut is chic or reminiscent of the 1960s. What those serious-minded folks may fail to realize is that a *nonstatement* of style is, in itself, a statement. I make no judgment about what is "good" or "bad" in style—that isn't at all the point. The point is that it is important to realize how your choices reflect your attitude. Whatever your attitude toward yourself and your surroundings may be, it is valuable to recognize that you are communicating a message to others, *and this self-expression reinforces your positive or negative self-image.*

Real style is not "put on" from the outside; it grows from the awareness of who you are and what you enjoy. It shows how you value the importance of the small differences that make each person special. You may discover great satisfaction in learning how to recognize the message your choices are communicating, and in finding new ways to reveal your tastes and interests—to celebrate your individuality.

Do you know which colors are the most relaxing for you to be around? Which ones make you feel irritated or anxious? During a seminar I presented at the Century Plaza Hotel in Los Angeles, a woman stood up and objected to one of the colors I had suggested in a relaxation exercise. The color was red—a color that is certainly *not relaxing* but was chosen as a balance to help people realize how sensitive they could be to specific colors. In a voice that reflected some strong feelings on the subject, she began to say how much she disliked "perceiving" that color. It had made her feel some very strong emotions that surprised her. Then she said, "I hate red, I really hate that color." The audience began to laugh and I could see that she didn't know why—not until I asked her to look at her clothes, and she realized that she was wearing a red suit!

Perhaps she wore the suit because it was a gift from her husband, or because it was on sale, or because a friend said it would look good on her. Most likely she just didn't know how much she hated red until she experienced the color in the Working Dream. Fortunately, she had a good sense of humor and was able to laugh at herself. Her experience prompted others to talk about their reactions to red, and then to other colors that had been suggested in the exercise.

A significant revelation to many that day was that color is a very personal matter. Yes, red does stimulate energy in most people (and sometimes anger), and soft pink is usually relaxing, and many people feel nervous around bright yellow. But it is also true that there are others who respond quite differently to these colors, and while it is valuable to understand the psychology of color as it is experienced by most people, it is even more important to recognize your own personal responses.

Colors, textures, styles, and details of clothing enable us to express our personal preferences. In a room full of naked people you would see little true manifestation of individuality. Bodies come in various shapes and sizes, but after you acknowledge that some people have taken care of themselves and others haven't, and that nature has not created us with equal endowments, what more is there to say? Naked bodies must rely on posture and movement to convey attitude and it is the choice of covering that most effectively conveys individuality.

Do you feel that you have a strong statement of style, or that you could develop it? When you have completed the following exercises you should know, or at least be on your way to knowing, several ways to enrich your life by being conscious of your own particular preferences.

Style starts from within and is manifested in physical choices. The self is expressed in a myriad of ways; critical to that expression is the knowledge of your loves and hates, needs and desires.

THE TRANSITION

Remember: You need your Working Dream notebook . . . a pen . . . a quiet place. Remember the series of events that will carry you into Transition as you close your eyes and experience again: a quiet beach . . . ocean sounds . . . the colors . . . the deep relaxation . . . your personal train . . . invisible tracks moving through space and through time. (Experience the feelings through memory or by reading again 19–24)

THE WORKING DREAM

The First Dream: Who Is that Person Living Inside Your Skin?

Follow the path that leads you into the stillness of a distant place, a place that is far from cities or towns. Discover that you are in a desert with soft dunes.

The sky is bluer than any you remember seeing since you were a child. . . .

Clouds shimmer against the richness of color . . .

The sunset is liquid gold.

Several places have been prepared for you and you may choose the one that is the most appealing. . . .

There is a blanket spread on the warm sand. . . .

There is a reclining chair. . . .

A hammock . . .

An outdoor waterbed.

Listen to the stillness. . . .

Watch the heavens. . . .

Know that only helpful thoughts will come to you in this place.

Twilight brings a darkening sky, the soft radiance of the moon.

Now the sky turns black, a velvet backdrop for billions of stars. . . .

Against the night sky the moon is luminous, ripe, larger than life . . . more beautiful, more perfect than you can remember.

The night air feels comfortable against your skin. Let yourself be enveloped by a mystical sense of space, of harmony with the universe.

Watch one special star that falls through the heavens . . . follow its path. Watch . . . and wish for wisdom . . . for peace . . . for love . . .
Wish that you might know yourself better. Wish for a clear understanding of your specialness.

To know your specialness, let Dreams play across your mind as you think now of something that fascinates you, some interest that is special to you.

Perhaps you wish you had pursued this interest further . . . or . . .

Perhaps you are feeling glad that you did.

Perhaps it is an old interest, something you wanted to do when you were a child . . . or

Perhaps it is a new interest, even something that occurs to you for the first time at this very moment.

Give your special interest a name and write the name in your dream notebook.

Fill the page with circles the size of biscuits. Inside one circle, write the name of something else that gives you pleasure. Fill the rest of the circles with anything that comes to mind that truly interests you.

Recognize the thought that attracts you most intensely at this moment. Write it in large letters somewhere on the page, or on the next page.

Whether you chose an interest in archaeology, music, theater, or a sport, or if you thought of a certain country you love and wished you knew more about, or if you want to collect rare books or antique toys, if you wished for *fewer* things because your world is too cluttered—whatever your wishes were, just be aware of them. Your wishes will reappear and be valuable in another Dream in a moment. Move on now, to this second Dream.

The Second Dream: Letting the Colors Choose You

Imagine, as you look into the heavens, that there are skyrockets shooting across the desert sky . . . first red . . . then orange . . . gold . . . blue . . . green . . . pink. . . . Watch them splashing across the sky, now washing the sky with color, as if the Creator of the Universe were wielding a wide brush and redecorating the sky.

Let the colors find you.

Keep watching the colors wash across the sky above you . . . any color on earth can cross this desert sky . . . you see a night rainbow, with its wild splashes of vibrant intensity . . . softer now . . . changing to any combination of colors that pleases you . . . perhaps even changing to beige or gray or shades of white.

Let the colors find you.

Let all of the colors fade, except one.
That is the color that chooses you.

Now add a color that seems to want to join with your first one.

Add a third, and soon you can see three colors that are
happy together and that you are happy seeing together,
here against the night sky.

And remember those three colors in your mind's eye, for we will
come back to them and they will have value in another dream in a
moment or so. Now you can move on to the third Dream.

The Third Dream: Redesigning Your Room

Imagine a room in your house (or in your office or in an imaginary
house, if you prefer) that you wish reflected your personal style.

Find yourself in that one special room.

In your Dream, you close your eyes and know that in that
moment the room will become empty, and the things that
were in that room will be kept safe in another place.

You are now free to explore the options that your imagination
suggests, as you create a room that is perfectly right for you.

In the Dream, open your eyes and see the room—first observe
the colors. Notice the color of the walls, the furniture, the carpet.

Choose a soft place where you would like to sit and run
your hands along the surface of the fabric. . . .
Feel the texture. . . . Is it smooth like velvet?
Is it leather or polished cotton, suede, or wool?
How does it *feel* to your touch?

Notice the style of the room. . . . Is it traditional or contempo-
rary? Are the pieces of furniture new or old? Have you had some of
them for a long time?

Look around the walls . . .
Is there sculpture anywhere?
Are there paintings?
Can you see them, or sense them, or know that even
though they are dreamlike you are aware of their colors and
moods?

Remember the words you wrote in the circles, expressing things that interest you. Are those interests reflected in any way in this room? If not, can you visualize how those interests could find some tangible expression in this room?

> In dreams you can have whatever you want. What do you want to see in this room?
>
> See it now.

Remember that many realities were, at one time, only a dream.

> While you are in this special place, this perfect room, and while you are feeling delighted with it all . . .
>
> Be aware that your body is just the size you want it to be.
>
> Enjoy the feeling.
>
> In your mind's eye, run your hands across your hips and your stomach and be aware of how you feel.

Imagine that you can watch yourself in the Dream. Your "dream ego" crosses the room, and your perception moves with your dream ego, and you look back at yourself, as if you are seeing someone else, sitting there. Let your dream ego observe the style of the clothes you are wearing and the colors you have chosen and the way you wear your hair.

> Let your dream ego watch while you walk around the room. How do you feel about seeing yourself at your best? Do you deserve to look the way you look in your Dream? Do you want to look like that in your "other" reality?

If there is anything else that you need to observe about yourself or your room, do it now.

> Now let your dream ego return to the self it has just observed.

In your Working Dream notebook, write down the observations that added insight into some aspect of your personal style.

Know that you can return to this Dream whenever it is appropriate to do so, whenever you want to do so. Allow only helpful experiences into this Dream.

THE DREAMER AND THE CRITIC

When you have awakened from the Working Dream and your Critic is ready to review its content, look back to the first dream. What do the thoughts inside those circles in your notebook reveal to you about your needs and your longings? Were there any new insights within the circles?

As you began to see the room that reflects your most intense interests, did you discover ways in which those interests could become a strong factor in your personal style? Perhaps you were able to experience colors more vividly than usual. You may have found some particular color that you want to keep around you in some way, just for the joy of it.

Personal Stories

A woman who hosted a popular television show asked me to lead her through a shortened version of this exercise while we were on the air. In the Working Dream she saw silk sofas, although in waking life she lived with cats. In her Dream, she wanted fine paintings, but in waking life she had a limited budget. What she gained from the dream was an awareness of how she would like to express herself through her environment. If she wanted to work toward actualizing her Dream in the waking world, some compromises would be necessary. Even so, it was extremely valuable for her to perceive the way her ideal room would look; just knowing the specifics of the Dream laid a foundation for choices she could make in her home.

Although she couldn't afford the original paintings she loved, she could afford lithographs by fine artists. Another way in which she might fill her home with affordable art would be to seek out relatively unknown artists, spending more time searching for the excellence she admired.

Ah, the cats. Well, what is there to do when you share living space with these recalcitrant cousins of jungle beasts? You accept some restrictions on personal style and acknowledge that *part* of your style is the priority you give to living creatures over tangible possessions. I know one woman who bought tougher fabrics because of her cats, and one who bought what she wanted and lived with the shreds. Another had her house-cat declawed—and chose silk.

I knew a girl named Sandra who loved to dance but had no great gift for it. She knew her limitations long before she experienced the Working Dream, but the Dream helped her see how dance could still be a valuable part of her life—and spontaneous associations occurred that gave her other insights, as well. She chose to fill her room with dance posters and reproductions of fine sculpture of dancers. Although she had chosen not to seek a career in dance, she became more aware of her posture and movement, and realized that she could, at least, *walk* like a dancer. There is a luminous transformation that comes over a young girl who suddenly becomes aware of bearing and body movement and the emerging of personal style.

Eliot Patterson has been fascinated by archaeology for a long time. When he entered this Dreamscape, he discovered that his study was covered with photographs of famous ancient sites, and of the archaeologists as they worked; he saw that museum replicas of ancient artifacts were displayed in a glass case along with small antique oil lamps. Later, in his waking life, it was not difficult for him to reproduce this ideal study in his home. That option had been available to him for years, but it hadn't occurred to him until he saw the room in the Working Dream.

I wish I could tell you that the pleasure he derived from the study inspired him to carry his Dream further, and that he spent one long vacation on a dig—but it's much too soon to know if such a thing will happen. Still, the thought has occurred to me, and so perhaps it has to him. Sometimes the expression of personal style becomes the catalyst for more significant changes in the way one chooses to live.

In this dream, Bruce Christianson, M.D., a gentle and delightfully philosophical psychiatrist, entered the den of his home and discovered that almost everything had been removed. There was a carpet on the floor, books in the cases, nothing more. Bruce felt comfortable in the room and said that it made him feel free of possessions. He would like to simplify his life and the room symbolized his desire to rid himself of the encumbrances of materialism. Later in the Dream, he imagined that he saw himself in that room and that he had become older and wiser—he had a white beard and seemed very much at peace.

Expressions of Yourself

Sometimes this exercise just reinforces the feeling that you are already doing exactly what you want to do about personal style. But if you gained new insights, make a note in your Working Dream notebook about what you learned from this experience. If there is anything you want to change or consider changing, write it down.

At the very least, these Dream experiences should have helped you focus on something that gives you pleasure and encouraged you to explore ways to incorporate it into your life. It may have taken you far beyond that simple awareness. If it awakened you to possibilities for expressing your personality more extensively, you'll recognize the value of returning many times to this Working Dream. The Dream can provide a lovely foreshadowing of changes for your waking life.

CHAPTER 8

RECOVERING FROM LOSS

There are no easy answers for dealing with the death or loss of someone you love. Grief is a complex matter and healing is slow and hard, leaving scar tissue that, for many people, remains tender to the touch all their lives. However, there are ways to cope with grief and with other forms of loss, ways that make the long nights more bearable and give constructive focus to the days. We can't avoid the pain of grief, nor should we want to; it is, after all, part of the fabric of our humanity. But we can choose to rebuild our lives, and to gain greater understanding of our emotions.

Notes from a Personal Journal

My friend died.

I don't understand you, God. I don't understand your time-tables—where the living dead live on and long to die, and one so young, so filled with life and love is gone.

I have to deal with sorrow in my own way—I try to race the pain, outrun the tears, rush past the anger and the loss—but the speed of grief transcends my need and leaves me spent and lonely still.

Now from this cold and silent place, I lay my grief before you to be healed. Though I can find no answers, help me to find acceptance. Though the pain remains, let the new day begin for me without bitterness.

The friend in this journal entry was my husband. He died one Thanksgiving morning without warning or a word. His death was caused by a heart attack and was unrelated to the fire that destroyed our home three weeks before.

The night before Leonard died we talked again about the fire and its impact upon our lives. We felt, as many people do when faced with this type of disaster, that it is only life that matters. I remember how much we talked about feeling grateful: No one was hurt; our children were healthy; our faith and marriage were strong.

At times, there was almost a sense of euphoria that came from the joy of being alive, and the awareness that our possessions did not possess us. So what if we didn't own a change of clothing or a coffee cup? We held our babies close and counted our wealth in love.

He had been at the office when the fire started. Because the flames moved so quickly, I had only enough time to get our children, the dog, and a book of photographs into the car. Our oldest child was two and a half; the baby was eleven months old.

In the months that followed, my journal entries reflected the shifting stages of grief, but this one awareness remained constant:

What can I claim as mine, Lord?
Not people, nor money, nor things—for all these can die or turn to ashes in the night.
So what is mine—except my feelings, my perceptions, and You?

The children are grown now. Time has given me perspective and yet, after all these years, the impact of that loss remains. I've been remarried for many years and love a remarkable man who is able to care for me without expecting me to "forget" the past. He adopted my children and loves them as his own. But in spite of all the goodness that has filled my life, in many ways I am a very different woman than I would have been without that loss.

Grief is complex, and when it has struck into the heart of our lives, we are never the same. In some ways we are stronger, in other ways more vulnerable. I hope that we are more sensitive to the sadness in others because we have learned to deal with it constructively in ourselves.

LOSS IS A COMMON BOND

There is an old Hasidic tale about a woman of great wealth whose child died and she went to a Wise Man of the village who was known to perform miracles. The woman offered to give away all of her wealth if the child could only be brought back to life.

The Wise Man told her that in order for her wish to be granted, she would have to journey through the land and bring him a coal from the fire of one house that death had not touched—a house in which no one, not master or servant, had grieved for the loss of a loved one.

The woman went from house to house, and at the end of a year returned to the Wise Man without the coal—but with a heart that had finally accepted the obvious fact that death is a part of life and no one is exempt from the sorrow that moves in its wake.

There are some feelings, some stages of grief, that are shared by everyone who has survived the loss of someone they love. Other feelings are more individual, shaped by the nature of the relationship with the person who died, as well as by personal resilience, spiritual strength, and a myriad of factors that give us our uniqueness. One chapter can't begin to deal with the complexity of grief—but we can focus on the attainment of peace within the struggle.

When We Want to Hold On

Every stage of grief is difficult—hardest is the letting go. This is true, not only for the obvious reasons of loneliness and loss, but because many of us have trouble realizing that we can turn loose of *grief* without turning loose of the person who has died. We can learn, in time, to replace mourning with celebration. Those words do not come easily; their meaning must be learned and relearned.

I know of no finer tribute to any love, than the celebration of all that was good and strong and nurturing in that relationship. This does not deny the tears and the sorrow. Neither does it ignore the reality that grief moves in erratic patterns through our lives; it is not a linear process. Just when we think it is finished, it hides in the shadows and lurches in the path of our happiness at unexpected times.

Anniversaries are always hard for some of us—for most of us, I suspect. For there is a whisper from some dark corner of our thoughts saying that what has happened once can happen again— as indeed it can. And so, fear is present too, and that makes it harder still.

But we can choose to let the celebration go on in spite of that. The celebration expresses the awareness that you can keep alive the good memories and call the hard ones by name. Face the rough times when they rise up to haunt you, know that you make the choice of which memories to relinquish and which to save. Celebrate what you had—and will always have; celebrate the past—and when you are ready, celebrate the future as well.

Other Kinds of Mourning

Grief comes in many forms and sometimes it has nothing to do with death. There are other kinds of abandonment that leave people feeling overwhelmed with loss. You probably know of several situations of this kind: marriages suddenly shattered when one person wants to leave and the other is still in love; relationships betrayed where once there was trust; even actions by a parent or a child that violate the human bonds. Between those who have suffered because they have loved, there is a common thread of grief— what is needed is a healing of the wounds and the decision to choose peace.

Denying the hard times, or running from them, hasn't worked very well for many people. But learning to face what was hard in the past, and to integrate it into our lives, makes us able to deal realistically with our feelings in the present.

But people must move at their own pace, and if you are still too tender, or your experience was too traumatic for you to work with imagery in this situation, then it would be well for you to pass over the Working Dream in this chapter.

At one of my seminars a few years ago, two women who were recent widows allowed themselves to experience an exercise that is similar to the one in this chapter and both told me how much it had helped them. One woman's husband had committed suicide, and she had carried a great deal of resentment, and there were many unanswered questions in her heart. Later, she said that the Working Dream was extremely healing and gave her a chance to say good-bye.

You are the only one who knows what is helpful to you in grief, and you must decide, by reading through the Working Dream, if it would be beneficial for you to proceed with this experience. This Working Dream is most effective for people who still daydream about the one they lost, and yet find that the daydreams only hold them to the past, preventing them from moving forward with their lives.

Any emotion that you feel can be used constructively in your life, if you face it honestly and choose to allow the feelings to give you insight. If the scene created by your Dream Maker is one of tenderness and closeness, you can choose to celebrate that feeling. If tears should come, remember that they can be part of the healing force; their purpose is to release sadness, and sometimes we don't use them as effectively as we might. Tears are part of the process of finding our way from mourning into peace.

Daydreams and Working Dreams should not be used to cling to what can no longer be; they should help us integrate the past so that the present is more bearable and the future more constructive.

THE TRANSITION

Remember: You need your Working Dream notebook . . . a pen . . . a quiet place. Remember the series of events that will carry you into Transition as you close your eyes and experience again: a quiet beach . . . ocean sounds . . . the colors . . . the deep relaxation . . . your personal train . . . invisible tracks moving through space and time. (Experience the feelings through memory or by reading again pages 19–24.)

THE WORKING DREAM

The Healing Journey

When you step from the train, you are deeply immersed in the dream, and you feel relaxed and positive about the experience that lies ahead.

> You are alone at the station and move toward the trail that will take you to a place of your own choosing. It could be a place that you associate with pleasant memories and with memories of the person you love—or you might choose a place that is mystical and soothing, where you have never been before.

Discover the path and notice what you see on either side.

> Be aware of the scents that fill the air and the colors that surround you. . . .

Listen to the sounds, or to the silence.

> Take time to experience how it feels to be in this place . . . . Find where you would like to sit. . . .
> Feel the peacefulness and let that peacefulness drift from the air into your body and thoughts and feelings.

Someone comes to greet you . . . this may or may not be the one you expected to meet in this Dream. Whoever has come to you has a reason for coming, and the reason is that you wanted to see this person again, for it was your longing that called this person forth from your memories into the present.

> You will see only what it is good for you to see and you will hear only what is good for you to hear.

You may choose to meet in silence. Many feelings are communicated in the stillness.

> But if there is something you want to say, say it now.

Take your time. There are many ways of communicating—you may hear the words or only sense their meaning; there are many ways of knowing.

If there is something you need to hear, hear it now.

Take your time.

If there are questions you need to ask, now is the time for asking—and for knowing the answers that are helpful for you to hear.

If you are angry, you can express your anger without fear of rejection.

If you need to ask forgiveness, or to offer forgiveness, let it be now.

Use this special time in any way that is best for you, that is healing for you.

If this person loves you, your well-being will be considered of great importance and you may be advised of ways that will help you deal with your loneliness and your grief.

In this Dream, love is not possessive and love wants only the best for the beloved.

Choose to hear the wisdom of love that wants only what is best for you. Let whatever is said and heard in this meeting help you to emerge stronger and more loving—and more capable of making wise choices for your life.

If you need to be comforted now, allow yourself to feel the unconditional Love that is available to everyone in the universe—to the weak and to the strong, to those who have loved and those who have failed to love. Allow all the powers of healing to encircle you, and from that Power take the peace and the strength that you need.

In your Dream notebook, write down what you experienced in this Working Dream. Begin with the last thing you felt. Write whatever associations occur to you now.

When you are ready, let your thoughts return to your workroom and let your mind slowly awaken from the Working Dream.

THE DREAMER AND THE CRITIC

This dream may have stirred deep feelings in you, even if the person you wanted to see has been gone for a long time. The past is as powerful as the present, so it is natural that your feelings may be strong. Keep in mind that the imagery was controlled by your Dream Maker, that this was "only" a dream. The words that were spoken to you were from the insights of your unconscious mind.

If your relationship with the person in this dream was very good, you may not want to analyze the experience right now. You may want to retain the dreamlike feeling for awhile and if so, you can consult your Critic at a later time.

Did the feelings that were expressed help you to realize that the person you love will always be alive in your memories?

If there were things that needed to be said or needed to be heard, ask your Critic to help you understand these realizations. Remember that you cannot "hear" any information that was not suggested by your unconscious mind.

If there was a great deal of new information that came to your awareness—or if there was anger or some disturbing emotion— you will need your Critic to help you use these emotions constructively. What do you think was the basis of the information or the feelings? Can you imagine why these thoughts and feelings would occur to you at this time?

If you created a healing Dream, you've used this experience to fulfill its finest purpose. If you brought forth hurtful information that needed to be confronted so that you can view the past more realistically, you may need to remind yourself that pain is often a critical factor in growth. Confronting negative feelings doesn't have to destroy experiences and feelings that were positive. But if you created a hurtful dream, and from it no positive value was realized, you may want to consider why your Dream Maker chose a Dream that would make you sad. You are, after all, in control of all of it. The direction of the Dream may give you insight into whether you *want* to be good to yourself and give yourself good feelings, or whether you are unconsciously choosing to intensify your pain.

And the Wise Man said: "Know the Truth and the Truth will set you free."

Write down your associations to this experience and read them again in a day or two, when you have greater emotional distance from the Working Dream. Find some insight in your experience that you can use to grow toward healing and toward peace.

Personal Stories

When Barbara Sax, M.D., a psychiatrist, opened her eyes from the Dream, it was easy to see that the experience had made a strong impact upon her.

The Healing Journey took her into a memory that had been painful for a very long time. Over a period of years, she had written to a special friend once or twice a week. Bob was a gentle and sensitive man, a confidant—and her husband's brother. They lived hundreds of miles apart and only saw each other at family gatherings, at which time they both felt shy and were never as open and communicative as when they expressed themselves in letters.

> In January of 1980 we were looking forward to a wonderful week-end when Bob's elder son was to be married, and my own son was to be an altar server. So many hopes . . . such joyous anticipation. But Bob had a massive coronary the week before the wedding and died within hours. The 'festivities' went on, preceded a few days before by the funeral. . . .

There had been no chance to say good-bye. No chance to explain why her letters to him had stopped. All that she needed to tell him would forever go unsaid—and she could only ask forgiveness of the silence that would be endless and unconsoling. And then there was the Dream. . . .

> As I step from the train, I am not surprised to find myself, not on a deserted beach or a mountain top, but walking up the street from my home, a steep hill to the crest of the peninsula where I once walked with Bob, and I am equally unsurprised to find him again

at my side. Some of the times we have been together we have been awkward and anxious, but this time we are both at peace with the world and each other. We greet each other quietly, and walk up the hill, our arms around each other, and there is no need for us to talk. Our smiles say everything and yet, there is so much more we want to say . . . and the silence is vibrant with hope and love. I hear his voice . . . 'How have you been?' (Not 'How are you?' as most people say).

We find ourselves in a meadow filled with spring flowers, poppies and everything colorful and free. We sit on the ground, face to face, our hands together . . . and again, we need no words. But I find myself telling him, 'I've missed you so much.'

Barbara went on to say the things that had been on her heart for such a very long time. She asked forgiveness for the letters that she had not written and for the silences that had come between them. She heard his words of forgiveness and accepted them, allowing his voice to dispel all the condemnation she had turned against herself.

When Barbara opened her eyes, there was a radiance about her face that spoke as eloquently as her words. The journey had brought the healing she needed and it is important to acknowledge here that *she allowed the healing to be complete*. It was finished. Since then, her memories of Bob are not tarnished by guilt, and she is able to remember him as he was in the Dream—and in life.

Mariam has many reasons to resent the husband she loved for thirty-five years. Although he had ample funds to provide for her, he chose instead to leave everything he had to his grown children from a previous marriage. Now in her sixties, she was confronted with a host of conflicting emotions that seemed overwhelming. Feelings of love were shattered by a sense of betrayal; misplaced trust made her feel ashamed. Rage coexisted with grief as his sons came into her home to claim half of everything she and her husband had collected over the years. (Although their personal possessions were not specifically mentioned in the will, his failure to exclude them meant they were now the property of men who had never accepted her as their father's wife, or as their friend.)

When they met in the Dream, Mariam's husband seemed as

real to her as any of the other characters she had met in Working Dreams. In her mind's eye, she could see him before her, sense his regret and bewilderment. He had never intended for his sons to take her home or any of the property while she was alive. They had promised she would never want for anything—and he had believed them.

In the Dream, he acknowledged that he had made a terrible mistake and grieved with her over what he had done. Because of the coolness between his children and Mariam, he was afraid that in her will, she would leave the money to her niece whom she adored; in trying to protect his children he had never meant for life to be so difficult for her.

She admitted in the Dream that she had enough to live comfortably if she was frugal, and that the greatest pain was not the loss of money but the symbolic loss of his love. In the Dream he wept with her and begged her forgiveness. And some would say she was wise and others that she was a fool, but in the Dream she forgave him.

I know (and surely you suspect) that she has repeated that Dream time and time again. Every time the rage starts, every time she has to see his children and feel again the shame. Forgiveness is not always easy, and it does not come to most people in one experience.

Someone who knows us both told me that he thought Mariam should have hated her husband. He said the Dream only perpetuated her fantasy of a marriage that wasn't nearly as idyllic as she seemed to think. Mariam could have chosen to hate him, or to forgive him; she chose to create her own perspective and to choose love. The Dream allowed her to accept healing, and it was in her nature to forgive—and to hold to the memories of being loved.

No Easy Answers

About a month ago, I had lunch with Gerald Jampolsky, M.D., and some others who had come to hear this extraordinary psychiatrist talk about releasing painful emotions through forgiveness. I remember he said to a man that day, "You can cling to being right—or you can have peace."

I'm glad Mariam chose peace.

The Price of Peace

Most of us have good logical reasons for the things that make us feel angry or abused. But what do we give up when we nurture these resentments—when we insist on being right and feel justified for our rage? Is peace of greater value—or is the price for peace too high? This is the choice that each of us must make. In the choosing, we select a way of life.

CHAPTER 9

FINDING PASSION'S WAY: COMPELLING CAREERS

———◆———

Blessed are those who have seen the inner dream and *know* what their life's work must be. Those who have the vision, and then make a commitment to the passion that drives them, are the golden few.

To know the name of your dream is one thing. To commit yourself to it, with all the frustrations and setbacks that are inherent in any career choice, is something else altogether. We can only imagine how many people head in the direction of the work they love, then turn onto a side road because of the misguided influence of others. Some have responded to the flirtations of a superficial desire, betraying their real love which, at some deeper level, longs to be fulfilled. The road not taken becomes a metaphor for dreams of what might have been.

We need to feel at peace with the choices we have made regarding our careers, or else we need to make new choices. To achieve wholeness, we must listen to the voice that calls to us from the dark room in our souls.

The process of Inner Vision is helpful when you want to get in touch with your dream and consider ways in which you can nurture it. It's possible that your unconscious mind already knows how to do that. The exercises in this chapter can help you bring those insights into conscious awareness.

It is also helpful to hear other peoples' stories. It's good to warm yourself by the fires of those who have succeeded in bonding their work and their passion to give creative meaning to their lives. Those fires radiate energy that can kindle new dreams—or even bring a dead or dying dream back to life.

WHEN THE DREAMER AND THE DREAM ARE ONE

His fingers stretched across the keys, and the synthesizer wailed a song both mournful and haunting. We were alone in the room. More accurately, Stevie Wonder was alone with his music and I, the observer, sat beside him, aware of the specialness of this moment. The power of his improvisation filled the room. It was raw emotion, a flight of images, a dream sequence. The music seemed to choose its own direction, progressing in mood, swelling in intensity. It started somewhere deep within him and poured out through his fingertips, moving through the keys, exploding from the speakers in the small room. Where did the music stop and Steve begin? I could not have told you at that moment, so compelling and hypnotic was the sound. The man and his work were one.

I thought of an exquisite quotation that the writer Charlotte Chandler attributed to Picasso in *The Ultimate Seduction:* ". . . you put more of yourself into your work until one day, you never know exactly which day, it happens—you *are* your work. The passions that motivate you may change, but it is your work in life that is the ultimate seduction."

Los Angeles Times Critic-at-Large Charles Champlin carried the thought even further:

> The real luck—and it is luck, an unsought and unbuyable gift—is knowing what your life's work and passion ought to be, discovering soon enough what seduces, and being able to commit to the relationship. Work is a demanding and frivolous lover, promising everything and not always delivering, turning frigid for no discernible reason (the empty canvas, the blank screen). . . . But

it's better to have a passion than not, and for all the frustrations that attend any form of creativity, it is as good a piece of fortune as the world provides: when your life and your work are one. It's that remarkable item, an affair that never ends.

WHEN THE DREAM COMES SOON

People who love their work are truly blessed, and they are even more fortunate when the dream is realized early in life. Stevie Wonder was a professional musician by the time he was ten years old. His mother, Lula Hardaway, told me she knew that music was his calling when he was still in his high chair. "Kids are always banging on the table with a spoon," she said. "But Steve was actually making music with his, even then." I don't doubt for a moment that he was. Perhaps it seemed to those who knew him that the music had chosen *him*, and his sole responsibility was to allow the gift to find expression through his life. Thank God nobody had a dream that Steve should grow up to be something else. No one placed his or her own concept of "proper choices" ahead of the choices that were Steve's alone to make.

It isn't only artists, musicians, and writers who are driven by this inner fire, whose love for their work is the compelling force in their lives. I suspect it's true for anyone who has found a way to make the work become an expression of the inner self. Bonding takes place when the work gives language to the silent longings of the soul.

Once upon a time, in the early 1930s, a small boy waited in the living room of his Michigan home while, in the next room, his grandmother lay dying. The doctor came and against all odds the grandmother lived. The doctor was paid in chickens and gratitude—and the boy knew, from that moment on, that someday he would be a doctor, too.

No one in his family was educated, and when the boy told them about his wonderful dream, they laughed and teased him about his high and mighty ideas. So the dream, the *knowing*, the passion to commit to his dream, was held secret from that moment until he finished college. He was twenty-three when he earned his M.D., and all through the years he never wavered in his sense of calling.

Few people have such a clear sense of purpose; those who do are the lucky ones.

WHEN THE DREAM COMES LATE

Even if the *knowing* comes much later in life, it is still magical, still a blessing. In the summer of 1984, in Pasadena, California, I visited Harriet Doerr, whose first novel, *Stones for Ibarra*, was published to critical acclaim when she was seventy-three years old. She had never written anything longer than a letter before she created that slim, exquisite manuscript.

I asked her if she regretted the years not spent writing. "I don't know if I could have started writing sooner," she said. "The thought didn't occur to me until the time was right. There are people who write and bring up children, but that must be terribly hard. I don't know how they do it. The interruptions are gigantic. Even with my husband, I wonder if this staying up at night and writing at odd hours of the morning would have been possible. I just don't know how I could have done it. It came when the time was right."

What a fine way of evaluating the selection of choices over the years. The day of our meeting, this vibrant, elegant author of a best-selling novel was preparing to leave for Stanford University where she would begin another year as a student in the graduate program for writers. There, she planned to begin her new book.

"I have to go away to get something written," she said in a strong, determined voice. "At home, I can't get away from the distractions. I feel something is missing when I don't write . . . I feel I'm just *part* of a person. Before I wrote I didn't notice that, but now that this part of me exists, if I'm not writing, I feel like I'm starving to death. It bothers me a great deal. I always think, next week the house guests will be gone, next week it won't be 104 degrees outside, next week. . . .

"Well, there are all these hands clinging at you, and you have to break away. The house clings, the garden clings, your friends cling, you have to cut through all that. But to do it feels terribly, terribly cruel. I try to say no. But it's so hard when nice people want something from you. I just have to get away."

Dreams do change, as time passes, for many of us. Priorities shift, and the most important thing is to be aware of the reordering of our needs so that we avoid working at the periphery of our lives. The writer's muse who now cries out for Harriet Doerr's attention wasn't even whispering in her ear during other stages of her life. When the time is right, inner voices have a way of making themselves heard.

WHEN THE DREAM MUST WAIT

There are times when passion for the work cannot be reconciled with circumstance or strong obligations. Sometimes, the price for personal satisfaction is just too high. The father of six young children, married to a woman who has no special skills in the marketplace, would be worse than a fool to quit his well-paying job to pursue an exciting but high-risk career. Sometimes dreams must wait.

Waiting is hard, but it's not as hard as quitting. Dreams die painful deaths, and just knowing that *later* you'll have your chance makes the waiting more bearable. One way to turn the timing to your advantage is to begin to prepare for the work you long to do. Then, when the time is right, you'll be far more knowledgeable and in a stronger position to create your own success.

Suppose the man with six children wanted to open an art gallery but accepted the fact that the timing was wrong. He *could* choose to wait until his children were grown and then make a career change. The intervening years could be spent increasing his knowledge and developing his own private collection of paintings. He might find that just working toward his goal could be extremely satisfying.

Passion has many stages, as any lover knows. And what isn't possible at one time may become a reality at another. If you doubt that collecting the work of others can be a strong personal dream, consider the words of a former curator of New York's Metropolitan Museum of Art, Thomas Hoving: "If there is one thing that all true collectors have in common, it is passion. What else is art collecting than a series of love affairs, each one as emotional, fulfilling, addictive, and shattering as the human kind?"

WHEN THE VOICE IS SILENT

Sometimes your personal muse calls out to you in positive, exciting ways and your direction is clear. Other times, that inner voice speaks through the pain of circumstance and sadness, calling to you through layers of discontent, begging to be acknowledged. And sometimes the voice is silent.

Silence can be a message in itself, advising you to move slowly, to look inward, to spend time focusing on what you *really* want to be doing with your life now and perhaps in five or ten years.

If you feel that the time is right for you to explore options and consider unconscious dreams, Inner Vision exercises will provide a fine means of transport into your inner self. Even when your work and your life are one, it can be helpful to wander into the deepest recesses of your mind and gain insights that can provide specific direction. For example, a writer might find the idea for a new book, an entrepreneur might discover a new way of approaching a marketing problem, an executive could gain insight into potential trouble spots in his corporation. When people open themselves to the inner wisdom of their unconscious awareness, they are gaining access to a part of the mind that is a rich storehouse for new and valuable insights.

THE TRANSITION

Remember: You need your Working Dream notebook . . . a pen . . . a quiet place. Remember the series of events that will carry you into Transition as you close your eyes and experience again: a quiet beach . . . ocean sounds . . . the colors . . . the deep relaxation . . . your personal train . . . invisible tracks moving through space and through time. (Experience the feelings through memory or by reading again pages 19–24.)

THE WORKING DREAM

Secrets from Beyond the Lagoon

Your personal train has taken you to a distant land, and as you move through the fog at the station you come to a beautiful place where the sun is warm against your skin and where flowers and green plants bloom in profusion. Their colors are exquisitely bright and the air is sweet with the scent of exotic blossoms.

A person you have never met before is waiting for you. You know that this is a capable and gentle guide who has been sent to help you on this journey. During this experience you will see what you are ready to see. . . . You will know what you are ready to know.

You are led down a path that is lush with tall grasses growing on either side, and you feel a sense of adventure and of trust. Know that you will experience only good feelings on this journey and it is perfectly safe for you to fulfill your wishes and your dreams in this fantasy.

Your guide takes you to a beautiful lagoon where the water is blue and sparkling in the sun. Perhaps you have been here before, in your fantasy. Amidst the lush foliage that encircles the lagoon, take off the clothes you are wearing and change to the bathing suit that has been provided for you . . . or you might choose to wear nothing at all.

Follow your guide into the warm water and be soothed by the pleasurable feeling of the water moving slowly up your body. . . . Enjoy the sensation.

Beneath your feet the sand is fine and soft . . .
Feel the shifting of the sand as you move.

Now the water is up to your shoulders. Feel the warmth, the gentle caress of the current against your body.

You are in charge of all thoughts and all feelings that come to you in this experience. . . .
You have great power and you will use your power wisely.
You are an adventurer to whom only good experiences will happen.

In this dream you can breathe and see underwater. You are an expert swimmer and you have the ability to swim to whatever depth pleases you.

If you want to, you can hold on to your guide, or you can just follow closely as you are led down into the clear, warm water.

Discover how easily you can breathe and see. . . . Without effort you can swim deeper.

Enjoy the sensation of the freedom to breathe easily under the water and the ability to see very clearly the small, colorful fish that swim nearby. Notice the vividness of their colors and the beauty of their movements and the peacefulness of the lagoon, here where no matter how deep you go the water is warm and gentle.

Take your time.

Now your guide leads you even deeper. . . . Together you swim toward a magnificent cave that is large and inviting and illuminated by shafts of light from an opening at the top of the cave. Trust your guide and the experience that is to follow. Your intuition tells you that there will be wonderful surprises.

Inside the cave is a world more beautiful than any you have ever seen before. . . . Take time to enjoy what you see before you move on.

Swim close to your guide as you go through an archway that leads you upward, then together you swim toward the surface of the water.

When you come back out through the water into the air, you see at the shoreline a world so luminous that you long to reach this exquisite place and to explore the wonders that you know exist in this special city.

You swim to shore with your guide and step out of the water. Your guide touches your shoulder and you discover that you are wearing clothes that are right for this place and for this time.

You are taken to the city that is built near the shore, and it
is more beautiful than any city you have ever seen.

Taking the path your guide chooses, and the means of transport
that is most pleasing to you, you find that with little effort and in a
moment of time you are in the heart of the city.

Someone very old and wise has come to welcome you and
offers you a warm and refreshing drink.

Take time to enjoy the experience. Feel the comfort and assurance
of the wise and caring person who knows you better than you have
ever known yourself. This person is known by many names: Coun-
selor, Highest Guide, Inner Advisor, Spirit of Love, Mentor . . .
and by other names, as well.

A Mentor is someone who helps you discover the best that is
within you. We will call this person, who has many names and
plays many roles in your life, your Mentor. Your Mentor now asks,
"What are the things you love to do most in life?" In your Dream
notebook write down the answers to this question.

Perhaps your Mentor knows of talents you haven't recognized, and may even suggest something. If so, write it
down.

And now your Mentor reveals that you will be staying in this city
for the duration of your dream, and while you are here you may
choose to discover the work that would give you the greatest satisfaction.

In this city there are people who create beautiful things.
There are people who build things.
There are people who take things apart.
There are those who work with their hands
and there are those who work with ideas.
Some of the people here find new ways to do things,
while others cherish and give new meaning to what is old.

In this place are all the things you need for what you want to do. (If you need to be in an area that is *not* a city to fulfill your dream, your Mentor will arrange that for you.) Prepare for your work, then, with a sense of adventure and confidence. Begin the work and experience the joy in the doing of it. Feel the satisfaction this brings. Know that the work you are doing in this dream is the finest work you are capable of doing. Feel the pride in your work.

Take your time. Enjoy the passion you feel for the work you are doing.

Observe the work and see that it is good. Concentrate on how you feel about what you see. When you are ready, write down what you have experienced while doing this work.

Know that you can return to this place and visit your Mentor any time it is helpful for you to do so. Here, you can explore options without risk.

When you are ready to return from the Working Dream, allow yourself to travel as you do in your most pleasant awakenings from sleeping dreams, moving gently toward consciousness, finding yourself once again in your workroom.

THE DREAMER AND THE CRITIC

There are many things you could be feeling at this moment: gratitude that even in the dream you chose the same work you have chosen in daily life . . . frustration that the work you want to do seems impossible at this time . . . excitement at a new idea, or the possibility that the idea can be transformed to your actual work. Or you may feel confused because even with the help of your Mentor your direction was not clear.

If your desired work is not possible at this time, imagine some things you might do to move toward that goal and make note of them. Think of this period as a time of preparation. If you did not receive a sense of clear direction in the dream, go back as often as it is pleasurable to do so and explore your options. Everything is not revealed in just one journey. If the work you really want to do seems appropriate for your life, consider what changes you would have to make to realize the dream.

What would you have to give up to make this dream a reality?

What do you have to gain?

What do you have to lose?

Would it be worth the price?

Would someone else have to suffer for the choice you want to make?

If so, would it be fair for you to act on your desire? Perhaps your answer is yes—someone may have made unreasonable demands on your life. Perhaps the answer is no—someone may seriously need your support, and a career change (which is rarely a lateral move) usually requires some sacrifices in the beginning.

Write down all the changes that would occur in your life if your new work is as successful as you hope it will be. If there is a high risk factor in what you want to do, consider the potential problems and how you would deal with them. Do you have the passion and the commitment to your new work that can sustain you through this transition? Do you have the discipline? Will the satisfaction of doing this work outweigh any possible disadvantages this choice may bring to your life?

It is wise to consider these questions in a dreamlike state when you have just emerged from the Working Dream, and then again later on, when your analytical powers are sharper. If you decide to alter the course of your life, do so only after reasoned consideration and great care. It *is* possible to fulfill your highest dreams when you have courage and passion—but you need preparation and discipline, as well. Move toward your goal using both your sensitivity as Dreamer and your judgment as Critic.

Personal Stories

This exercise has led some seminar participants to make dramatic changes in their careers. Because the Working Dream puts the dreamer in touch with his or her unconscious desires, people are often surprised to discover that they are walking through life on a road that will never lead to their most satisfying choices. Some entrepreneurs have perceived that they would be happier in corporate life, and a few corporate executives dreamed of starting businesses of their own.

It's been interesting to see how many people who experience this Dream sense a strong feeling of responsibility toward "higher goals." In one session, Bruce Christianson, M.D., psychiatrist, felt that he was being led through the lagoon by a ball of golden light that seemed to represent a Higher Power. His Dream contained an interesting metaphor: The work he chose to do in the city was to invent something that proved to people that lying was not a viable solution. All lies would be revealed as deceptive as soon as they were spoken—and soon people would realize that there was nothing to gain from lying to each other; they would have to find an honest way to communicate. People, and then nations, would see that lies had no value and peace would not seem such an impossible goal. The Dream only reinforced Bruce's commitment to help people achieve a higher standard of ethical behavior in their personal and professional lives.

Dominic Molloy, who designs computer programs for an accounting firm, attended that same session. He dreamed that he invented a game in which all participants worked together to create the perfect game. There were no winners or losers, and all facets of the game were used to improve the society. The game became the main pastime in the city. The game was about global responsibility; it was about caring and helping others and when he came out of the Dream, Dominic said that he realized he would be much happier in a job in which he worked for the betterment of society—even if it involved a significant reduction in salary.

Sensing that he had left the dream too soon, Dominic felt that he wanted to go back to the Dream on a different day; there was more that he wanted to learn in the city of the Dream.

For some time, Helen Pankowsky, M.D., has questioned the choices she made regarding her profession; she enjoys psychiatry and works primarily with disturbed children and their families.

Even so, something does not feel right, and she has been trying to gain clarity on the direction her life is taking.

During this Working Dream, when her Mentor asked. "What are the things you love most to do in life?" her answer came immediately: "I like to teach, to write and to paint."

Although she had been struggling with this issue for some time, when Helen experienced the dream she felt no ambivalence in her response. It was obvious that one of her options would be to teach psychiatry at a medical school; writing and painting could be enjoyed at her leisure, not as a vocation, but as a satisfying hobby. But Helen sensed that the answer was not that simple.

She had always been torn between medicine and the arts. In addition to that, Helen is a spiritual person and believes that there is some "calling" that has eluded her; she has started taking classes at the Jung Institute to pursue a more spiritual direction as a therapist. No matter how it seems to others, Helen perceives herself as a woman in transition, with many career questions still unresolved.

As we talked about her love for writing, she became animated and then, suddenly, her voice lost its soft, wistful quality and, in a much harsher tone she told me that she didn't know if she had the talent to be a writer. Her self-criticism seemed to take the joy away from the fantasy she had just experienced.

Helen was quick to admit that she needs to find a way to avoid the negative attitude her personal Critic has created through stern and unloving judgments. She also seemed to feel anxious about her indecision, as if she had to discover the answers right away. I sensed that her desire to take a specific course of action might block many good ideas yet to come. So I encouraged her to take time, to "live the questions," to use the months during which she is studying child psychiatry to explore options for her future—without eliminating any plans that she currently had in mind.

To keep her Critic at bay, she agreed to give herself permission to play with her insights without expectations. I suggested that she buy an attractive box that would hold colorful dividers—and the writings and drawings she collected. I showed her the ones I use in my "writer's notebook." She could imagine that this box contained a collection of personal treasures, like the shells one might collect at the beach. Rather than trying to work with her collection of writings and sketches, she could play with them as a child plays with a collection of shells—or stamps or paper dolls. Giving the inner child permission to play, without imposing judgment, can keep the stern Critic from overwhelming a fragile dream. What is important now is not that Helen make a firm decision, but that she allow her Dreamer to maintain proper balance with her Critic.

A woman with Helen's expertise has many options: It may be that she will decide to teach psychiatry when her special studies are completed. Or she may use her training as a springboard for her writing, using her education to enrich the content of her work. She might combine her talents as an artist with her psychological insights and write books for children that could help them deal with difficult situations. We have discussed many possibilities and Helen agrees that her first goal is to give herself permission to wait for a clear sign from her unconscious before she makes any changes in her life.

Your Personal Choices

Whether this exercise helps you discover new insights or merely reinforces what you already know to be true, it should provide an uncommon setting in which you can explore your feelings.

Honor the longings that emerged in the Working Dream, in any way that is right for you. And take your time. Remember that this dream can provide additional insights each time you return to it. In every reenactment, your discoveries will be different. Decisions that will affect you for the rest of your life deserve several encounters between the Dreamer and the Critic.

CHAPTER 10

TAKING A FIFTEEN-MINUTE VACATION

If you were invited to go anywhere in the world you wanted to go, stay at the hotel of your choice, travel by the most sophisticated means of transportation, return to work without experiencing jet lag, and it wouldn't cost you a thing, what would you say?

This invitation can be extended through the courtesy of your rich and generous imagination, which is limitless in its capacity to think up fascinating activities for you to experience.

Because most people feel too much stress and not enough pleasure, and have too long a stretch between holidays, I designed "The Fifteen Minute Vacation." It was created as a survival tool for those who need a quick, refreshing experience for both body and mind.

Tension is important and often constructive in our lives; it warns us of danger, pushes us to excel, and is critical to success in many ways. It's the degree and the frequency of stress that cause people trouble. One way to benefit from its value and avoid its danger is to learn to control its presence in our lives.

Even when your work gives you a deep sense of satisfaction, there comes a limit to physical and emotional endurance. I use some variation of the exercises in this chapter almost daily (and several times a day when I'm working under a tight deadline or unusual pressure). The exercises not only provide a minivacation, but they are also invaluable for stimulating right-hemisphere activity that contributes to the creative process.

When you can break away from your work and take a flight of fantasy in the Working Dream, you are able to perceive your problem from a new perspective. You can *play* with the situation and allow fresh and innovative ideas to come to mind. You can break out of traditional approaches and discover the creative ideas your unconscious mind has been aware of all along.

Once I used the exercises in this chapter with a private client who was trying to learn how to stop overreacting to the pressure of her job. She discovered that her irregular heartbeat (premature ventricular contractions caused by a mitral valve prolapse) settled down into a normal pattern when she used the exercises every day for a week. To my surprise and hers, her doctor took her off heart medication and months later she was still able to control her problem through imagery.

Not all heart conditions can be helped by this process. *If you are being treated for any medical problems, you should never stop taking medication unless your doctor recommends doing so.*

But the result of other medically tested programs involving imagery indicate that in many cases blood pressure can be lowered, muscular tension eased, and pains that are both somatic and functional can often be reduced or eliminated. This is true for a variety of techniques that teach you how to use your mind to create a healthier body.

VACATIONS IN THE MIND

Many corporations have policies that encourage their executives to take time off on a regular basis. Many people in less nourishing work environments find it more difficult to get time off, even though they recognize the need for a break from pressure and routine. The ability to take a minivacation in your imagination, without taking days off from work, allows you to come back refreshed and with a new perspective. It's also a delightfully entertaining mind-sport providing an inexpensive and enjoyable holiday.

Choosing the Best of Where You've Been

Using the Working Dream, you can *experience* any memory of any place you've ever been. If you want to go back to your favorite beach, you can return in a blink of your mind's eye. You can feel the sand against your skin (in fantasy, you can eliminate the crowds and the sunburn). You can swim the warm waters (and not worry about jellyfish or barracudas). You can have the best of it all—and you can have it as many times a day as you need to "get away."

Choosing the Best of Fantasy Trips

Vacations in the mind provide an experience that feels quite magical. A pilot in one of my seminars found that the cost of keeping his own plane was getting out of hand, and he had to give it up. He could rent a plane, which he did on occasion; this gave him great enjoyment but did not replace the pleasure of having a plane of his own. During a Working Dream exercise, he discovered that he was able to fly without a plane and had an experience of great joy and release when he soared in the richness of the dream.

People who have formerly participated in sports that are now beyond their abilities find these fantasies particularly pleasurable. Skiing, deep-sea diving, sky-diving, hang-gliding, and other activities for the lion-hearted can be wonderful, accessible experiences in the safety of the mind's imagination.

Learning to Play Again

High achievers, and those who would like to be, often have difficulty remembering the importance of play. The inner child can cry all night for attention and not be heard above the roar of daily responsibilities and ambitions. There's value in the fantasy that allows you to escape from the reality of life for fifteen minutes (or longer, if you can spare the time).

Four vacations are suggested here. The first takes you to a private beach, the second to a place behind a waterfall in a tropical lagoon, and the third takes you to a ski run high in the Alps. The fourth dream transports you to a place of your own imagining, a place you have been to and to which you want to return, or a place you have never been to but which you can create in your own fantasy. Two of the exercises involve the sensation of flying, which creates a feeling so exquisite that it is the absolute favorite of all those I use in my seminars.

THE TRANSITION

For the exercises in this chapter, you don't need to go through the Transition experience introduced in Chapter 2. Some of the techniques in that exercises have been incorporated into this first Dream. You will need your Working Dream notebook, a pen, and a quiet place.

THE WORKING DREAM

The First Vacation: A Private Beach

You are walking on your private beach which glistens with white, finely-sifted sand. You walk along the edge of the gentle waves, seeing that for miles and miles you are alone.

> The sounds you hear are the sounds of the waves which begin to build far in the distance. . . .
> Listen to the deep rumbling sound of the sea . . . the wave that rises to the surface of the waters, white and foaming, racing toward the shore, and the sound of it is different now—lighter, more playful—and the sight of the waves is wondrous, the white water glistening against the blue. The wave moves closer and then dissipates in a whisper of faint, effervescent sound as the foam explodes with fine bubbles that burst and merge with the wet sand, golden and fine.

Sit down and listen to the ocean and follow the image and the sound of one wave and then another . . . then another . . . keeping your eyes on each wave and observing its details, and hearing only the waves and the call of a distant sea gull, and feeling the

sun, warm and relaxing against your body, and the breeze, soothing and refreshing on your skin.

Feel the sand shift beneath the weight of your body, forming to the contours of your body, and watch the clouds
stretch streamers of white across the blue sky.

You can see a rainbow arching over you, soft colors turning vibrant when you want them to. The rainbow becomes a kite that
sails across the heavens, its streamers purple, red, and orange,
yellow and emerald green. The rainbow-kite flies above you as if to
entertain you for a while.

Now the kite becomes a mystical bird with magnificent
feathers that spread out against the blue sky, bringing good
fortune to all who see this gentle, wondrous bird in flight.

Time moves erratically in dreams . . . from one season to another, one cycle of the sun or moon to another. . . . Notice how
the sky has turned dark and the stars shine brighter than you have
ever seen them, and the air is warm like a summer night.

You watch the stars, and the clouds that shadow the moon
and move on . . . now the moon is full and you watch the
images across its surface . . . pictures shift on the face of
the moon.

Lying there, you allow your mind to drift aimlessly, feeling your
body so relaxed in the sand, feeling the air like a light blanket of
warmth covering you, listening to the sounds of the gentle waves.

Realize now that time has passed without your awareness,
that you wandered into a deep dream that lulled you
through the night, and notice now that it is just before the
dawn and the sky is lighter and the stars are barely visible in
this morning twilight.

Now the sun has awakened the world and you are alive with the
energy of your visions.

Remember how the bird with the rainbow wings emerged in your imagination and how it flies by the magic of your thoughts, and know that if you want to, you could fly by that same magic of imagination, and nothing could hold you back except your own perceptions.

Knowing that your imagination has endowed you with great powers, you can, if you want to, let your body rise from the sand in the quiet of the early morning, and fly away from the beach. . . .

You can fly over a vast jungle, seeing beneath you ribbons of vines strung throughout the trees . . . there are myriad shades of green and trees of varying heights. . . .

And then you fly further, past the jungle, over mountains, and rivers. . . .

Perhaps you see cities you have never imagined before, and you see beauty more wondrous than you have ever imagined, and you rise above these sights to an even higher place where you rest on the wind and feel the greatest relaxation you can imagine.

Feel as light as a butterfly, riding the warm currents that carry you safely to the place on the beach where this journey began.

And you now make a choice: You may come out of the Dream or you may continue on to "The Second Vacation: Behind the Waterfall." If you want to come out of the dream and return to work, then you will gather great sources of energy into your mind by willing it with your thoughts. Now you can feel the positive energy that refreshes you and prepares your mind for clarity of thought and vision . . . and you feel the energy that has come to you from the flight of fantasy.

The Second Vacation: Behind the Waterfall

Imagine that you are in a beautiful setting in the mountains, in a place that is warm and inviting. Follow the trail that leads you through green trees and beside a stream.

Cross the stream and climb higher to where you can see a waterfall cascading from still higher levels of rocks, a waterfall that is so inviting on this warm day that you seek the cool waters of the small lagoon beneath the falls.

You make your way along the path that leads to the lagoon.

You may want to take off your clothes and place them on a large rock by the water's edge. Know that you are safe and in a secluded place where no one can come without your invitation.

You step into the water, and the temperature feels perfect against your body. . . . Swim toward the falls and feel the shower of cool drops on your face and then stand in the shallow waters below the falls.

You might feel like exploring further, and if so, you move behind the waterfall where you can hear the sounds of the falls and see through the curtain of water to the green path you followed to come to this place.

The lagoon is deeper here, and you realize that if you could dive down, you could explore all kinds of rich opportunities. And as surely as you could fly with invisible wings, you can swim underwater and breathe underwater in that same magical way.

Swim down into the lagoon and see how exquisite the world is. . . . Play among the small colorful fish, the stones, and crystal rocks on the sandy bottom.

Play in the water in any way that you enjoy.

From some distant time in the past, a pirate's treasure has washed up into the lagoon and the jewels sparkle in the clear waters. If you want to, you can take a handful back with you, but be sure to leave some for others who may come after you and want to enjoy their beauty, also.

When you are ready, come back to the shore of the lagoon where the sun and the warm air will dry you before you put on your clothes.

When you are dressed, rest a moment in the coolness of the ferns and rare flowers. Then you can either move on to the next vacation or generate the energy you need to feel alert and ready for work; then return to your workroom.

The Third Vacation: An Alpine Ski Run

In your mind's eye, create the vision of a winter haven, where the world is blanched white and the silence is deeper than silence can be in any other place on earth.

You walk along the path in your down jacket, with the hood pulled over your ears, your hands in leather gloves lined in cashmere, your feet in warm boots that lock out the moisture and the cold of the snow along the trail. The air is cold on the surface of your skin but it doesn't seem to penetrate into your body, for you feel warm inside, and the cold rests lightly upon your face, and your body is warm from the feel of down and cashmere.

High in the mountains the stillness calls to you, and in this place only peace seems possible.

Look at the vista before you: the mountains, white and glistening in the sun, stretched out like slumbering dinosaurs with their backs humped toward the sky . . . irregular forms all white and soft reminding you of . . . clouds . . . powder . . . fur . . . dreams . . . silence . . . peace . . . eternity.

You see the trees ladened with new snow. . . . In the distance, there are small houses and perhaps a lodge, a haven where you are welcome.

The path has led you to the top of the ski run, and skis and poles that are perfect for you are waiting there. Whether, in the waking world, you ski well or not so well or maybe not at all, you have every reason to believe that in this Dream you can ski without effort because the skill is all in your imagination.

Now the skis are on your feet, clamped securely, the poles are in your hands and you find that it takes no effort at all to start the long trail downward. You travel at the speed you choose, and you follow the trail that is right for you.

The trail curves and you move so easily with it, feeling the freedom . . . wondering why you ever thought it was hard . . . thinking about your good fortune at being here in the snow . . . in the mountains . . . in the crisp, dry air . . . in the silence . . . and the peacefulness.

You stop to rest and to listen to the silence, to enjoy the stillness . . . nothing is moving, even far away in the village . . . there is peacefulness everywhere.

Start again down the trail and you can move as slowly as you like or as quickly as you like, for you will choose the trail that is right for you and the speed that is right for you.

Ahead of you is a jump which you may choose to take if you want to, for you have no fear of the jump. . . . You are totally in control and nothing will happen here in this Dream without your consent. So, if you want to, you can jump and feel your flight into space and the free, soaring experience of the jump and, because all thoughts are magical in a dream, you can choose to land or to continue your flight, sailing over the trees and trails toward the small village below.

You can fly on your skis . . . then prepare to make a safe and easy landing in the flat space at the bottom of the run. . . .

When you are ready, come down the mountain to the village and your haven.

Go inside and leave your jacket and your boots by the door and cross to stand by the fire. Smell the cedar and the scent of eucalyptus leaves in the fire, and there is the aroma of hot soup or cider on the stove.

Perhaps someone is waiting for you . . . or perhaps you choose to be alone . . . the choice is yours.

Sitting by the fire, you close your eyes and feel grateful for this place that you can visit any time in your imagination.

And you decide whether to move on to "The Fourth Vacation: Returning" or whether you want to return to your workroom by letting your mind fill with energy and carry you back into your waking reality.

The Fourth Vacation: Returning

Using the skills of imagination you are learning and perfecting, take yourself to a place you have been to before, in a situation that is ideal for you, to which you have longed to return.

Notice all the details of the place: the temperature of the air, the colors you see, the things around you. You can enjoy all the smells and tastes and textures of this special place just as you enjoyed them when you were here before.

Are you alone or did you bring someone with you?

Choose the things you want most to do, the things that called out to you from this place in memory. Relive the memories you want to relive. . . .

Change the memories you wish were different. . . .

Be aware of all that is good in this experience and hold it closely in your heart. Give yourself all that is positive and helpful, all that is beautiful and fine.

Take a moment to wonder why you chose this place out of all the places you have been. Know that you take with you from this experience what is best for you to take, and you will leave behind what is not nourishing for you to carry with you.

You are mastering the powers of your imagination and your creative forces. You can choose now whether to remain longer in the dream or to come out of it, feeling that your body and mind are refreshed and renewed by this experience. When you are ready, let your thoughts carry you back to your workroom.

THE DREAMER AND THE CRITIC

If you were working on a difficult project, or struggling with a troubling personal matter before you experienced these dreams, you may be surprised to find that you have gained greater clarity as a result of the deep relaxation you experienced.

Because these particular Dreams were suggested to you to be used for relaxation, you may not have been expecting any messages from your unconscious. But since we can never be sure what will happen in the unconscious mind when we are in this relaxed and receptive state, it's important to be aware of the possibility that insights may have been revealed to you in metaphor or even in undisguised forms.

If insights came to you during these vacations, count them as blessings, remembering always to feel grateful for the serendipities in life. Remember that while all you consciously sought was a small vacation during your busy day, you should also welcome gifts of insight, for they are jewels to be examined by your Critic before you move on.

Personal Stories

Many people have told me that when they are under pressure at work they find it difficult to set aside even fifteen minutes for themselves. These same people admit that when they discipline themselves to take the "minivacation" they feel refreshed and their work is often enhanced by the process. Even so, they often feel guilty for taking time to do something so playful when serious business is at hand.

I don't know anyone who practices Inner Vision techniques who doesn't struggle with this conflict at some time or other. Most of us are conditioned to believe that the quickest way to a solution is to press on straight ahead through the problem. We don't easily realize that a circuitous route is often more effective.

Making Time

If time justification is a problem for you, imagine you're with a team of workers tunneling through a mountain made of rock. The shortest way from point A to point B is a straight line—right through the mountain. The quickest way, however, is to walk around the mountain where others have gone before and shown the way. It's not only more expedient, it lets you have time to enjoy your journey while you're en route to your goal.

CHAPTER 11

MOVING ON

---◆---

When you think of the words *moving on,* what associations come to your mind? Do you think of changing careers, or changing houses, changing habits, or changing attitudes?

The words will have different meanings to you at various times in your life but there are certain questions that will be useful to consider no matter what your particular situation may be. When you move on, you always need to consider what you have to gain and what you have to lose, what you want to take with you, and what would seem intolerable to leave behind. Those considerations are valuable whether you're moving up in your career or preparing to move on into retirement. They are equally relevant to more personal decisions. These are important questions that should be asked of your *feeling* self as well as your *thinking* self.

I'll tell you a story about a woman who moved up (in her professional life) very quickly, and another about a man who planned his career change for years. And in the stories that follow the Working Dream, you'll see how the Dream that leads one person to move across the world will inspire another to write a poem. I wonder what the Dream will inspire in you and what changes you might make in your life because of it.

SUDDEN CHOICES

In the summer of 1984, when I was a guest at Stobo Castle in Scotland, a London journalist named Leonora Langley was also visiting there. Thinking back, I remember our conversation at tea one afternoon, when she spoke about how much she enjoyed her work and yet sensed that she was preparing herself for some change in the direction her career was taking. We talked about imagery, which she used often, and although it was a pleasant day and I enjoyed her company, I had no premonition that we would meet again, or that there would be any connection between my work and hers.

A few months later she called from the Bel Air Hotel in Los Angeles and asked if I would meet her there for dinner; she had been sent here to do a story on the hotel and would be in town only a few days. At dinner, she talked about how much she had enjoyed her stay in Los Angeles and how fiercely she hated to go back to London. I listened to her experiences in this tough and power-structured American city and thought that in two weeks she had met more celebrated and controversial people than most journalists interview in months. Her voice dropped when she talked about returning to London. The obvious question anyone would ask was: "Then why go back to London? Why don't you stay?"

"Oh, I couldn't possibly!" Leonora said quickly and there was an anxious laugh that curled up after itself in a minor key and settled down gently on the next sentence. "One can't just take a trip and *stay!*"

All I asked was, "Why not?" and the rest of the evening was a matter of listening, making mental notes, and asking a few obvious questions. We had planned an early dinner—I had a seminar to lead the next day, and she had an interview with Jackie Collins. As it turned out, we were almost the last ones out of the hotel dining room and somewhere between the soup and the fresh raspberries, Leonora's life was turned in a most intriguing direction.

Because she was experienced in doing imagery, Leonora could enter the Working Dream with her eyes open, sitting up at the table, with only a sixty-second Transition exercise. I led her into a Dream in which she lived in Los Angeles, experienced the different rhythms and moods of the city, saw the challenges of this luminous/bewildering/bewitching town which is, in many ways, the antithesis of London. She anticipated some periods of loneliness, recognized that there were challenges and risks involved in the move. She considered the things she would have to give up to come here: old friendships, familiar patterns of daily routine, a well-established reputation in her field, easy access to the people she wanted to interview.

She considered the challenges: the fear of loneliness—she was a stranger in a hard town to crack; the fear of failure—what if she couldn't get through to the celebrities who formed the cornerstone of her livelihood?; the fear of success—unknown temptations and unexpected pleasures stir both longing and anxiety in most people.

In her mind's eye she imagined calling her mother and sister to say that she was staying in California; in her fantasies her mother accepted the news well. Later, in her associations, Leonora told me that years ago her mother had said she thought England was restricting for such an ambitious woman and she had encouraged Leonora to start fresh in California. (I wonder how many California girls have been sent off to Europe by mothers expressing the mirror image of that thought.)

Leonora realized that it was her own "need to be needed" that had led her to intensify the bond with her mother, to become her protector and in many ways to form a symbiotic relationship. Now that Leonora was emotionally able to break the dependency, she realized that her mother had an ample support system and, for the first time in her life, Leonora had the right, and the opportunity, to just take care of herself.

As a Features Editor of *Avantgarde* magazine, Leonora could work from Los Angeles as easily as from London.

She had a flat in London she didn't want to give up—just in case things didn't work out for her here. How could she arrange to keep it and not pay double rent? Leonora didn't miss a beat before she suggested that her sister loved the place and would surely be thrilled to move in. She could also ship the clothes and any personal items Leonora felt she needed right away. One by one, we eliminated the problems that stood between Leonora and her dream—even to the lawyer she might see to deal with immigration problems.

In only a few hours, Leonora made the decision to stay in

California. The first few months proved difficult—filled with anxieties and confrontations with the daily problems of life in Los Angeles. But in less than a year she was working as an editor on *The Hollywood Reporter* with her own Friday column and byline. She was also sending stories off to European magazines and leading a social life that most native Angelinos only dream about. About that time, *Avantgarde* magazine folded, and if Leonora had stayed in London, she would have been looking for a job! She moved "over and up" as the result of a Dream.

MOVING ON SLOWLY

It isn't often that a person makes up her mind so quickly to move halfway around the world. Most people take a long time to decide to move across town. Usually the process begins unconsciously, the Dreams reveal some disquieting material, there are hints of unrest and wishes begin to emerge along the horizon of the Dreams.

I have a client in London who is the chief executive officer of a major international corporation. He was formerly president of three other firms before this one and is well connected in international circles. We happened to see each other in Davos, at the European Management Foundation's Symposium and I noticed how many presidents of corporations and countries made their way over to say hello. His position seemed well established in the fast-thinking world of international business and politics.

We began working together in 1983—first in London, then in Los Angeles. Sometimes he would fly to Los Angeles for an imagery session on his way to the Orient or as an extended weekend when he was in New York. Always, his Dreams centered around his need for change—and for challenges not related to the world of business.

He said that he was mentally preparing himself for retirement, which he believed one should plan for as seriously as one plans for a career. He wanted to start investigating communities that would be intellectually and spiritually stimulating. He thought of Santa Barbara, California, or La Jolla to the south and asked me to arrange some introductions for him there. Probably the essence of what he wanted was to someday consult for a corporation that recognized the holistic needs of the employees and to implement programs to enrich their personal and professional lives. He anticipated that he would make his move in five years.

In 1985 there was a major upheaval in his corporation, and against apparent odds, he lost control of the firm. It was a shattering experience for him and he felt rejected by a company that had expanded solidly and broadly under his leadership. There was a great deal of publicity, which he handled well for a proud man who is extremely visible in the business community. But there was a high cost to his spirit, and it showed when we met in November of 1985.

We are friends now, as well as business associates, and I met him at the airport when he flew in for a few days of imagery. It was the first time I observed any signs of jet lag, and his confident demeanor was tinged with greater vulnerability than I had seen before.

As soon as word was out that he had left the London firm, offers began to come to him from all over the world. He had many options, all of them from major businesses where he would be doing the same sort of job as before, confronting the same kind of challenges, experiencing the same type of frustrations. He longed for something more stimulating, more related to higher values and human potential.

We worked together during four days of intense Inner Vision sessions. At the end of each day, he would choose one Working Dream that he felt was most important, program himself to dream about its meaning in his sleep that night (a technique he learned from *The Right-Brain Experience*), and the next morning he would rise early so that he could spend an hour or two re-experiencing the Dream on his own.

Although some might consider that much concentration on one exercise to be excessive, the proof of its value is in the results: During the four days of Inner Vision work, he had clarified his own needs and specified exactly what he wanted to do about his career. He would contact a Swiss firm that had wanted to work with him for years, and offer them a program for executives of large international firms which would include the type of nourishment he longed for in his own life.

Human needs do not emerge in vacuums. This man believed there were others who would respond to his ideas because they had felt the same emptiness in their own lives. It is obvious that financial success and power do not equate with inner peace, and an increasing number of business leaders have begun to recognize this.

He called the Swiss firm immediately and set up an appointment to meet with them. He left Los Angeles charged with great energy and excitement; he was to present his program in Geneva one month later. *Moving On* for this man will be the personal/ professional Dream consolidated and brought to reality. He has clarified his goals, envisioned his success, and taken responsibility for his perceptions and his actions.

This man's story would be inspiring no matter what its specific outcome. But the result makes the telling of it even more exciting: He called from Geneva to say that he had sold the idea to the Swiss firm and that his first conference would begin in the Fall of 1987. One of the Dreams that had the greatest impact upon his decision is the one you will experience in this chapter.

THE TRANSITION

Remember: You need your Working Dream notebook . . . a pen . . . a quiet place. Remember the series of events that will carry you into Transition as you close your eyes and experience again: a quiet beach . . . ocean sounds . . . the colors . . . the deep relaxation . . . your personal train . . . invisible tracks moving through space and through time. (Experience the feelings through memory or by reading again pages 19–24.)

THE WORKING DREAM

One Hundred Caves

Your train has carried you into a bare and distant land, high in the stark mountains that reach far above any known civilization. Notice the warm terra-cotta color of the earth, the feel of the hard clay beneath your feet. Be aware that you have come here to discover something that is important for you to know.

The trail leads you upward, and as you climb higher, notice the primitive formation of ancient stone structures, where once a great people lived before they moved on.

The trail leads you to a place where you can see a hundred caves in the mountainside. There are large caves and small ones, some easily accessible, others more difficult to reach. In the past, people lived in those caves, and you can sense how one might have lived a fine life in this place, for there is an aura of peace and tranquility, of history and of personal passages. In this civilization, great lessons were learned and you might feel that some of this wisdom can be transmitted to you, in some indescribable way.

As you look at the caves, there is one in particular that draws your attention. This cave seems familiar, though you can't imagine why. It may contain secrets; it may reveal something that is important for you to know. Something about your present circumstance is associated with that cave.

Notice that there is an easy way to get to this cave. Take the path that leads you there and when you enter the cave pay careful attention to everything that you see in that place.

Now look at the relationship of this cave to the other caves that exist in this cluster of dwellings. Is your cave surrounded by others or does it stand alone? Is it small or large?

Let this cave represent your present and the memories of your past. Let it contain all the wishes and dreams, the assumptions and perceptions, that you have acquired all through your life.

In your Working Dream notebook, write what you see and what you feel about this cave.

Nothing stays the same; everything is in a process of change. You move on in subtle ways or dramatic ways, in gentle transitions or in sudden awareness. You will not stay the same—and you can choose to invent your future.

> Stand at the opening of your cave, where you can see the multitude of caves before you. When the time comes for you to move on, where would you like to go? Is there one cave that stands out as the best of choices?

If you were to move on to this new place, there would be things that you would need to take with you. (Perhaps courage, and a sense of adventure.)

> There would also be things you would need to leave behind. (Perhaps some old habits, or attitudes.)

Soon you will move on to the new cave. What will you want to take with you when you move? Make a note of your ideas in your Working Dream notebook.

> What will you want to leave behind, possessions or habits or attitudes?

> Make a note of those thoughts, as well.

Take the path that will lead you to the new cave. What do you see in this new place?

> What is the relationship of this new cave to the others?

How do you feel in this place?

> What are the challenges here?

What are the risks?

> What are the pleasures, the rewards?

Is there anything you need that you don't have?

Can you provide it for yourself?

How do you feel physically?

How do you feel emotionally?

How do you feel spiritually?

Are there any surprises for you here?

Stay in this cave as long as it is nourishing for you to do so, as long as the secrets of the cave are being revealed to you.

If you would like your Mentor to appear to you in this place, let it happen now.

Ask any questions you need to ask and hear any answers that are valuable for you to hear.

Make use of your time in this mystical place in any way that is helpful for you.

When you are ready, slowly bring yourself back to your workroom and open your eyes.

Make note of any insights you want to remember.

THE DREAMER AND THE CRITIC

As your Critic helps your Dreamer assess the insights from your Dream, maintain a curious mind and an imaginative attitude; the metaphors expressed in this dream may be extremely important to you. Everyone is in the process of moving on, in one way or another. This Dream should help you understand more about the way that is right for you.

In your waking life, have you been thinking about any particular aspect of moving on? A new job? A new relationship? A change of city? Transitions within yourself? What do the feelings you experienced in the cave reveal about your feelings in waking life, regarding your longings, your desires (or fears) about moving on?

In sleeping dreams, and in Working Dreams, caves and houses are metaphors for the inner self. What did your caves reveal about the way you feel about yourself?

Were there surprises for you in this Dream? If so, perhaps your unconscious mind has been planning some changes in your life that have only now been revealed to you.

Personal Stories

The psychiatrist Helen Pankowsky, M.D., who has struggled with the challenges of moving to Los Angeles, had a revealing experience in this Dream. She visualized the caves as if they were situated in the plateau country of the American Southwest; the sandstone caves resembled the ruins of the *Anasazi* (The Ancient Ones) that were once the home of Pueblo Indians. Dramatic and mystical, these abandoned ruins appeared to Helen as elegant metaphors for the transitions she has been experiencing since she came to California.

In the first cave, Helen had a feeling of familiarity and safety, but the cave seemed bare and incomplete. The second cave was accessible only by a tall ladder that rested securely against the sandstone cliffs. Inside, all associations to a real place and culture had vanished: The walls were painted a soft lavender color, there was a fireplace, a handwoven rug, flowers in a clay vase.

Helen had a good feeling about the place and it seemed as if she belonged there. She was concerned that perhaps the ladder would fall, so that she would be isolated from others. She checked the ladder and found that it was securely anchored against the wall of her home. She was also concerned that the cave would be cold, so she put another log on the fire. Looking out over the other caves, Helen felt glad that she could see where she had come from, but she had a strong desire to stay in her new home.

Physically, she was warm and comfortable—emotionally, she was at peace. Spiritually, she felt close to God, as if she had been led to this place for a purpose.

When she talked about her associations to the Dream, Helen felt the metaphors were obvious: She now feels that Los Angeles is her home, and although she wants to keep ties with her past, she feels good about her move. In effect, she has *already* moved on and her transition is complete. She realizes that new cities can be lonely for women alone, and when she put the log on the fire in her Dream, she was, in fact, recognizing that she has the power to create the "temperature" of her environment. Her house will be cold only if she fails to use her resources for making it right for herself.

Helen said, "Anywhere can feel like home, if you want it to. After all, your home is really within yourself."

When she had this Working Dream, Helen had already begun working on the illustrated story she thought about writing in "Finding Passion's Way." She had also (finally!) put her California license plates on her car—and bought a huge canvas to paint a picture for her living room. She came to our meeting wearing a magnificent lavender sweatshirt elegantly hand-painted with an abstract swirl of color and beaded with crystals. California has had its impact. Helen has carved her home out of the raw material of Dreams. She has also worked hard at changing her perception, and the rewards for her efforts continue to nourish her.

The psychiatrist Mary Christianson had a Dream that was quite different from Helen's and provides a fine example of how to alter the Dream suggestions to create your own unique experience.

Think back to the Transition exercise . . . and remember the suggestion of a warm sun and clear blue sky with clouds. Mary's Dream Maker had other ideas for her this day: She sat in the reclining chair and watched the storm clouds blowing toward the shore. Thunder rumbled in the distance and she huddled in her blanket to ward off the cold wind blowing in from the sea.

"My train comes just as it starts to rain," she said. "I love the warmth of my compartment and the storm raging outside. I listen to the thunder, watch the lightning and everything is intensified, somehow more vivid than memory can ever be.

"My train speeds through the desert and then leaves the tracks and soars high above the earth, and then it feels like a glider, landing finally at the station in some primitive place. I see the caves but I don't want to go into them. I take another path that leads down into a meadow—there are variations of green and yellow, bananas growing on trees.

"The path leads to the ocean and I see a hut which is my new home and it has a thatched roof. It isn't raining but beautiful, dark clouds are forming. Inside this home there is a fireplace, bookcases, a rocking chair. I can hear a Mozart sonata coming from the stereo. There is an easel with paints and brushes. There is a bottle of wine and glasses, but I'm alone there. People are outside; I can hear them and I know they will come in if I invite them. For now, I'm just enjoying being alone."

The Dream was extremely satisfying for Mary and she was impressed by the changes that have occurred in her attitude since she began working with the Dreams. Earlier, she would have told you that she was extremely conservative in her personal choices. Even in the Dreams, she would "test the territory" before she went all the way into the experience. Now she was impressed with her ability to "float" into the situation without trying to anticipate what was coming next.

"I was self-conscious at first—always worrying beforehand about what I would say or write down in the exercise. Now I feel free of all that—free to experience the Dream in a different way than it was presented—free to allow surprises and not be threatened by them. I don't have to be in control all the time. It's as if I don't have to *know* what will happen.

"What I left behind me was my fear of new situations, and the need for security. What I took with me was the phrase, 'You don't always get what you want, but you always get what you need.' "

Although Mary felt that she had given up control in the Dream, she actually was exerting strong control as she resisted the suggestions and chose her own way. She felt like she relinquished control only because her conscious mind allowed her unconscious to take over during the Dream.

All of these experiences have had a profound effect on Mary, as she has wanted to move beyond the safe confines of her traditional background. Every session, she commented on the fact that she was the Doubting Thomas, the skeptic. I think she has been amazed each time we've met that she is increasingly able to explore her fantasies, learn from them, and then make concrete changes in her life as a result.

For Mary, the theme of *Moving On* is not an issue of changing cities or careers or relationships. *Moving On* refers to the inner growth that is taking place as she explores options, changes perceptions, and considers the choices she wants to make for her life.

Mary's resistance to the suggested imagery is an interesting example of how you can make the Dreamscape work for you in any way that you choose. Every group has people who prefer to alter the imagery—and of course there are others who never want to tamper with the suggestions.

When I was teaching at the Santa Barbara Writer's Conference last year, I led the group from a "mental massage" where all their tight muscles could be mentally relaxed by a magical masseuse who entered their Dreams. From that image, I suggested that they "put something on" and then board the train with the others in the room, each in his or her private car. Soon the cars became animals and the train was a parade that moved down a steep canyon toward an adventure in a hidden city.

One woman told me after the Dream that she had been terribly frustrated: She had imagined that she got up from the massage table, put on a robe, and rode the train into the desert. When the car in which she was riding turned into a horse, she was upset because I hadn't told them to dress appropriately for riding—and she was bobbing around on the horse without wearing a bra! For her, this was no minor problem and she said that, although she wanted to go on with the Dream, she couldn't enjoy it because her robe blew in the breeze and she was miserable without her bra.

There are good and obvious reasons why it is sometimes necessary to adjust the Dream suggestions to your personal needs. Everything you need for the Dream can be provided by your imagination—all you have to do is wish for it and it will appear.

Barbara Sax, M.D., has shared her Dreams in several chapters. You will remember her as the psychiatrist who last appeared in "Recovering from Loss." In this Transition, Barbara said that she also made a change in the suggested imagery: The steel tracks had always seemed like an intrusion upon the beauty of her spectacular beach, so in this Dream she imagined that the tracks were sand-colored and therefore invisible. She saw this as a metaphor for a new perception—that she chooses to be less controlled by her environment. She has the power to make more changes than she had realized before.

In the cave, she knew there were rooms she couldn't see; they were not frightening, but she knew that she was not ready to go into them. It was winter in her Dream and the cave needed more light. She was concerned about people getting to her—would they know (or care) that she was there? She experienced a poignant feeling within the cave and again realized her desire for poetry, for music—and for new clothes of brilliant red. She experienced an awareness that somehow in the cave the spiritual, poetic side of herself would be nurtured. The Dream seemed to be a reinforcement of earlier Dreams, in which she confronted her desire for more of these qualities in her life.

For Barbara, I suspect that *Moving On* is a critical issue, for there is a restlessness of spirit that is apparent in this elegant woman with her quick wit and perceptive insights; in most people this quality of "aggressive seeking" precedes an important shift in life's direction. As of this writing, Barbara is "living the questions."

Bill Champlin (who is unrelated to the other Champlin mentioned earlier) is a studio musician, sings and plays keyboard for "Chicago," won a Grammy for writing "After the Love Is Gone," and received two gold records for "Chicago 16" and "Chicago 17." He found this exercise to be particularly moving. The cave, while confining, opened his awareness to the vastness of a universal plan. For Bill the highlight of the experience was the sensation of a pure, radiant light that was the essence of Love. The light was pure Spirit; all else fell away. He had a sensation of moving from the confines of the first cave into a vastness of space, encompassed by the light that was so incredibly nurturing.

For Bill, *Moving On* is a process that he takes most seriously. Changing habits and addictions (minor or major) are difficult for everyone. Bill has made his commitment to live free of alcohol and drugs and imagery is one of the tools he uses to reinforce his resolve.

Bruce Christianson, the psychiatrist who perceived of himself as an old man with a white beard in Chapter 7, "Discovering Your

Personal Style," (pp. 85–95) experienced the first cave as his life at this time, and the second cave as life after death. In the second cave, he felt that he had made the transition to a higher level of existence where his life continued in a more glorious form. More than anyone in the control groups, he took the instructions literally and lived the Dream to explore the broadest perimeters of his life. For Bruce, *Moving On* provided a spiritual journey into the future.

A Gift for You

It is interesting that so many people become aware of their own spirituality in the Working Dream. Some people become conscious of a void—or they experience a presence that surprises them. Often, those who haven't considered themselves even remotely spiritual begin to notice an awareness of a Higher Power.

Allow the message of this Dream to be a gift to you from your unconscious. Challenge any suggestions that distress you—and learn from the insights that follow. Use the Dream in any way that will benefit you and make your life more rewarding.

CHAPTER 12

LOVING COUPLES: CONFLICT, COMPASSION, AND COMMITMENT

———◆———

In all the surveys I've seen that attempt to compile what is important in a loving relationship, communication and empathy rise to the top of the list. Each of us needs to feel understood; we want to know that the most significant person in our lives is willing to listen to our point of view and to have compassion for what we feel. Of course, we must provide that same empathetic loving action for our partner. The words are so easy to say (and have been written about so often) but there is nothing facile about the doing of it. In fact, of all the Working Dreams in this book, none require greater maturity or motivation than the one in this chapter.

Of course, it's easy to listen and to empathize when your partner is sharing feelings about situations at work or with others, but if the words coming at you are in conflict with your own position and if they threaten you by their implications and if they hurt you or anger you or make you feel misunderstood, you will find that empathy is not so simple after all.

It's hard to resist the urge to defend our positions or explain our motives, or accuse the other person of wrongdoing when we feel misunderstood ourselves. It's hard to *want* to listen when what we really want to do is express our own views convincingly.

Loving, lasting relationships between equals require that both partners develop the skills of listening (when they would rather talk) and experiencing compassion and understanding (when they would rather that their partner was having compassion and understanding for them).

GIVING UP MAKE-BELIEVE

Where is it written that true love lives blissfully ever after? And who said that there are no conflicts or rages or tears when love is "real?" We learned it first from all those childhood fables that slipped their lies into our expectations. There was Snow White and Cinderella and all those Doris Day movies and a whole society telling us that Love cured everything. (Indeed it does, but not in the way that was implied in the happily-ever-after tales.)

In the spring of 1984, I was seated next to Leo Buscaglia on a plane from Los Angeles to Washington, D.C.. Since he is one of America's most prolific authors on the subject of the dynamics of love, our conversation moved to the subject of relationships. He told me a story about his parents whose marriage was arranged in Italy in the early 1900's before they came to America. Theirs was a marriage that lasted for 63 years and contained a great deal of laughter and a fair amount of tears and once Leo asked his mother if they had ever considered not staying together. He quoted her indignant reply: " 'Divorce?' Mama said, 'Never! Murder, often! Divorce never!' "

When love is real it is not always blissful; loving couples do not always agree—neither do they pretend to feel what is not felt. But when love is real, it sustains. It makes a commitment to the partnership that mandates fairness and compromise and it radiates light through the dark caverns of misunderstanding by its commitment to endure. When love is real we don't have to be afraid to be who we are—to reveal ourselves in our vulnerability—because we know that we will be cherished in spite of our weaknesses. When love is real, it leaves each person's uniqueness intact.

One cannot write fairly about commitment without addressing straightaway the fact that some unions are destructive to one or both parties involved. Sometimes people must go their separate ways. In *Loving Each Other*, Leo Buscaglia wrote:

> We are not evil, inadequate or incompetent when our relationships fail. It may have been that we were simply overconfident about them, not adequately prepared for them or unrealistic in our expectations of them. . . . So, if a relationship becomes destructive, endangers our human dignity, prevents us from growing, continually depresses and demoralizes us—and we have done everything we can to prevent its failure—then, unless we are masochists and enjoy misery, we must eventually terminate it.

I've known two couples who terminated long relationships with such kindness and regard for the other's feelings that many people who knew them wondered why they broke up. They never spoke unkindly of the former partner or referred to a "bad marriage." One woman said to me, "I can't imagine destroying the memory of twenty-five lovely years by focusing on the pain of the last five."

Those who need to terminate their relationships will not find condemnation here. But those who love and are "committed to the concept of commitment" may find this Working Dream provides nourishment for a relationship that is growing and ready to spread its roots in deeper soil.

NEGOTIATION: ONE OF A LOVER'S MOST IMPORTANT SKILLS

Roger Fisher, Professor of Law at Harvard Law School and director of the Harvard Negotiation Project, wrote in his book, *Getting to Yes*, ". . . The ability to see the situation as the other side sees it, as difficult as it may be, is one of the most important skills a negotiator can possess." I would say that is also true for any lover, or anyone at all who wants to heal the wounds that misunderstandings have inflicted.

When Roger Fisher and I were both speakers at a conference in Switzerland we spent a few hours discussing the role imagery could play in helping people understand each other's positions. He told me that imagery has been used in the Harvard Negotiation Project and that it has worked well in terms of helping people perceive not only the other person's point of view, but in understanding their own perceptions more accurately. "Conflict lies not in objective reality, but in people's heads," he wrote in *Getting to Yes:*

> Truth is simply one more argument—perhaps a good one, perhaps not—for dealing with the difference. The difference itself exists because it exists in our thinking. Fears, even if ill-founded, are real fears and need to be dealt with. Hopes, even if unrealistic, may cause a war. Facts, even if established, may do nothing to solve the problem. . . . As useful as looking for objective reality can be, it is ultimately the reality as each side sees it that constitutes the problem in a negotiation and opens the way to a solution.

Roger has negotiated with the leaders of many nations and helped them understand the other's point of view; he also negotiated for the release of hostages in the 1985 Beirut hijacking crises. But I'm sure the basic premise in negotiating with powerful nations, fanatical terrorists, or with a single couple, is the same: individual perception of the situation is the pivotal issue.

THE GIFT OF EMPATHY

Once there was a couple who had been together for many years and who never raised their voices in anger. They always stopped short of the full truth of their feelings in deference to the feelings of the other. Differences were buried beneath the smooth sands of courtesy and one day an issue came between them that couldn't be denied and they shouted at one another and said hurtful things and they felt isolated by their rage and defenseless against the current of accusations that lashed between them. And although they loved each other very much they were both afraid, for they had never learned how to deal constructively with their anger and they were like lost voyagers in a foreign land who didn't know how to find their way home again.

Neither of them knew what to do until things were so bad that they cried together and held each other close and agreed that no matter how much they disagreed about the issue between them they would not stop loving each other and they would walk safely together through the crisis. What kept them together where others would have parted was not only the fact of their love but the fact of their commitment to their relationship.

In an experiment that was difficult for each of them, they agreed to be open to each other's pain and to accept what the other had to say. He offered to be the first to assume the role of "active listener" and during that time, when she described the depth of her feelings without reservation, he didn't argue nor explain; neither did he try to change her mind. And when she had said everything that was on her heart, it was then her turn to listen to what he felt and she provided the same nurturing situation for him to express his point of view. She didn't argue or explain, neither did she try to change his mind.

When he had said all that he wanted to say, they each entered the Transition on their own and each encountered the Working Dream. They remained in the same room, but they took their separate journeys into the Dream. In the preparation, he acknowledged that he could separate himself from his own perception for the duration of the Dream, knowing that this would not commit him in any way to her position.

In the Working Dream, as much as he was able, he encountered the affect of their differences as she had experienced them, using her own words as his guide. And he was able to feel compassion for her and to empathize with her and for that short time, her vision was absorbed within his own and he understood. He made notes of his feelings during the Dream and he wrote down the insights that came to him. And then he left the Dream and returned to his partner.

And she did the same for him—preparing her mind to receive his feelings and releasing her own position, she entered the Transition and the Working Dream. And as far as she was able to do so, she perceived their differences from his position. And when the time came that she felt compassion for him and empathized with him, she wrote her insights in her notebook and return to waking reality.

When they came together, each expressed what had happened during the Working Dream and they shared their new insights and agreed that there was not just one true story here but three: the way he saw it and the way she saw it and the way it probably was.

And then it was their responsibility to decide how they would respond to each other's needs. And they kept in mind her feelings and what was best for her, and his feelings and what was best for him. And they also kept in mind an image of their relationship—as if it were a living thing apart from themselves that needed to be nurtured. And they agreed that no decision would be made that would destroy that relationship.

And in the course of the Inner Vision experience they negotiated a solution that was for the benefit of the couple and which allowed for the needs of each of the partners. Later they looked back and wondered why it had ever seemed so complicated and so hard.

RULES OF THE GAME

This is the first exercise in the book that involves using the Dream with another person and a few things need to be said about that. People are extremely vulnerable during and after the Working Dream (as you know by now from your own experience) and it is important that neither person ever takes unfair advantage of this vulnerability. To be most effective, both partners need to realize that this is a tool for bringing them closer together, not for one to gain an advantage over the other. When both partners share a commitment to the relationship itself, the Dream can bring them closer. When both people do not share this commitment (or if one is uncomfortable with Inner Vision techniques), it is helpful to use the Dream alone, without the other partner's participation. You can benefit from these insights even if your partner is not yet prepared to enter the Dream.

The Working Dream is based on the concept of role reversal that has been used for some time in various forms of psychotherapy. The advantage of using Inner Vision is that you encounter your partner's feelings when you are in a state of deep relaxation and your own defenses are at a minimum.

SETTING THE STAGE

Since this exercise is basically designed as a tool for resolving conflict, imagine that you and your partner are discussing a subject where there is no agreement. If you have been together very long, you have probably realized that "real" love (like real life) contains frustration as well as ecstasy. Choose an area of conflict and recall everything your partner has said about that situation. (This will be important in the Working Dream.) *Do not rehearse your own feelings about the subject at this time.*

THE TRANSITION

Remember: You need your Working Dream notebook . . . a pen . . . a quiet place. Remember the series of events that will carry you into Transition as you close your eyes and experience again: a quiet beach . . . ocean sounds . . the colors . . . the deep relaxation . . . your personal train . . . invisible tracks moving through space and through time. (Experience the feelings through memory or by reading again pages 19–24.)

THE WORKING DREAM

The Gift of Love

When you step off your personal train, you are in a small, deserted station high in the mountains of a faraway place. The path that you follow leads you through beautiful woods and you listen to the silence and feel the stillness. Be aware of the slow and easy rhythm of your breathing. Smell the fragrance of the forest.

The trail turns and soon you see a house that is wonderfully pleasing to you. You know it is all right for you to be there and you walk up to the door and step inside.

Within the house is a chair and the chair is soft and inviting. Perhaps there is a fire in the fireplace. Make yourself comfortable here, in this quiet room where you are very safe and feel extremely relaxed.

Because you have expressed your pain or anger or frustration and know that you have been heard, you do not have to defend your position during this Dream. You are free of the burden, here, in this peaceful place.

Take a moment to experience a sense of freedom from the attitudes that have separated you from the one you love. Let that feeling be acceptable to you now and let your understanding, compassion, and empathy be a gift of love that you give to your partner and to the relationship you share together.

Recall the words your partner spoke and let the words enter your consciousness as if they are your own thoughts, as if the feelings belonged to you, as if that vision of the problem is, for this moment, absolutely true.

Take your time.

Stay with the feeling until you can perceive the situation as the other sees it. Do not run away from what is important and true from the other's point of view.

Do not analyze the feelings. Accept them and let them exist in your mind without question.

Perhaps you will suddenly understand why these feelings exist. If these insights come, they will come to you effortlessly and you will understand. Or they will not come to you now and you should not try to call them forth.

There are other things that your partner said about this problem that have come between you. Consider them now. Allow yourself to feel what your partner feels.

Take your time. Accept whatever feelings come to your mind without argument, without defending against them.

If you are having difficulty getting in touch with these feelings or thinking these thoughts and you need help, call your Mentor forth and discover your Mentor in this room with you, bringing wisdom and assurance.

And if you want to, and if you ask, your Mentor will enable you to experience how your partner feels, in that simple way that Dream Mentors have of fulfilling what the Dreamer truly wants.

If you want to, you could even imagine that your body becomes weightless, invisible, free to merge with the one you love, becoming one in spirit, one in feeling. In this transformation you can imagine the feelings, the longings, from that unique perspective. And although it is not possible to totally understand what another person feels, this can bring you closer to understanding. . . . Now you can feel your partner's pain and that pain becomes your own and you feel compassion and empathy and you feel the vulnerability the other has felt and the feelings are as real to you as your own pain was real to you before.

Take all the time that you need.

If there is anything you want to ask your Mentor that will help you clarify your thoughts, ask now.

And if there is anything you need to hear that will enable you to understand more fully, hear it now.

And again you can imagine that you are weightless and invisible and that you return to your own self. Remain in that quiet state, with your new perspective and your feelings of love, of forgiveness, of empathy.

Write down all the insights you have gained so that you will not forget them, for they could slip from your awareness like the images in a sleeping dream.

When you are ready, bring yourself slowly back from the Dream to your partner. When you have both returned from the Dream, share what you have experienced. You do not have to resolve anything at this time. You do not need to negotiate or to defend. Let each other know that you understand—that you have compassion for the other's sadness.

Take time to be loving.

Take time to feel peace.

THE DREAMER AND THE CRITIC

When you have assured each other of your love and your understanding, you are ready to work toward a resolution of your problem. For the next few moments, continue in the role reversal by listing what you would be unable to do (or to give up) if you were the other person and then list what you would be able to give up if you were the other person. Present your case as effectively as you can from the other person's point of view. You do not need to do this aloud, if that seems threatening, but you can do it in your notebook.

You may feel that you are arguing against your own position but in fact you are arguing in favor of the relationship of the couple and you don't need to worry about defending anything right now.

Write down the new insights that came to you during the Dream. If any feeling was particularly strong, continue to write about it and write your associations to it until you feel that you have explored all that you are able to explore about that situation.

When you have finished and you are both ready to work on the resolution of your differences, you will come together with increased awareness of each other's feelings. Then consider not only your partner's best interest and your own best interest but also what is in the best interest of the couple.

If you have entered this Inner Vision experience alone because your partner refused to try, or was psychologically unable to try, you may feel a deep sadness at this moment. You have assumed the responsibility for both partners by exploring a possibility for healing—you have entered alone where the couple was not prepared to go. Give yourself comfort by acknowledging that this was a gift of love from you to your partner and from you to the relationship and also from you to yourself—for at this moment, even though there is sadness, is there not also a new strength and fullness of love that nourishes you? And don't you feel stronger for having the courage to explore the imagery? We can hope that as your partner observes the change in your attitude as a result of the experience, a change of heart will follow—and perhaps soon you can enter the Working Dream together.

Personal Stories

When Karen and Dan sought out Inner Vision techniques in conjunction with the traditional marriage counseling they received elsewhere, they were optimistic about the outcome. She was experienced in imagery and used it for many situations in her life. He was less comfortable with the process than she, but nonetheless willing to try, and his attitude was positive.

Basically, their problem existed because of painful situations each had experienced prior to their marriage: Dan's mother had abandoned him when he was two years old and no amount of love or logic had convinced him that he would not be rejected again. He had a great need to control the finances in the family and to be sure that Karen remained dependent on him for her livelihood; he didn't want her to work, seeing this as a move toward independence, and therefore toward the day when she would leave him.

Karen, on the other hand, was afraid of dependency. She had never had a job and was terribly afraid that the day would come when she would have to provide for herself and would not be able to do so. The more she sensed his controlling attitude the more she was threatened and the greater her need to take care of herself.

And of course, the more he sensed her pulling away from dependency on him, the more threatened he felt and the more determined he was that she should stay at home with the children and leave the breadwinning to him.

In the Working Dream, she entered his childhood through fantasy. She imagined herself in a crib, crying for a mother who didn't come—who never came—and imagined the series of homes and adjustments and the feeling of abandonment and insecurity. She imagined herself in his place in their marriage, unconsciously wondering when he would once again be deserted by a woman he loved and needed. And when the Dream ended, she understood why he resisted her moves toward independence.

Dan entered the Working Dream, placing the time as a few years before they met. Karen had married early, straight out of high school, and her first husband had inherited a great deal of money. They lived quite well, and it never bothered her that she had no money of her own. When he chose to be with another woman, Karen did not want to take money from him but had none of her own and no education or skills for the marketplace. As much as he was able to do so, Dan "tried on" the feeling of vulnerability that he knew Karen had experienced. At the end of the Dream, he had a good sense of what Karen had been feeling and why she was so afraid of her feelings of dependency.

An awareness of these feelings enabled both of them to feel compassion and empathy for the other. They also had a better understanding of how their individual problems interplayed to threaten the other partner. Everything did not become rosy just because they had the intellectual understanding and the emotional awareness of their situations. Months of therapy would be required before real healing would take place. But the Dream united them as a team and their resolution was strong. The Dream gave them a depth of compassion and a commitment to their marriage that they had not experienced before.

Working with the Dream

If you and your partner decide to use this Dream for enlightenment, remember that one session of Inner Vision isn't likely to solve problems that took years in the making. You may need to encounter the Dream on several occasions before your perceptions can change. Self-help books rarely espouse the need for patience but false expectations can only set you up for trouble. Working with two people is harder than working with one; and couples in conflict will do well to let the Dream provide a means of gaining understanding, while recognizing that these insights cannot cure the conflict until each member is prepared to compromise for the sake of commitment—for the sake of love.

CHAPTER 13

BONDING AND SEPARATION: THEMES OF PARENTING

◆————

I was a good mother then—when all the baby needed was love, a full breast, and a dry bottom. I was a good mother later when she toddled around her circumscribed world needing attention and a watchful eye. But now she's seventeen and I don't know what she needs but I'm sure it isn't me and I'm not sure at all what being a good mother means.

I remember writing those thoughts in my journal a few years ago and I recall the feeling of helplessness that engulfed me on so many occasions during my children's adolescent years. Bonding had come easily to me—separation was far more difficult. And so it is for many of us.

Last night a friend told me that she had put her arms around her seventeen-year-old son and kissed him on the cheek a few nights before he left for Europe to spend a year as an exchange student; he said, "Mom, please . . . I'm trying to separate, and you're not making it any easier."

Unfortunately not all teen-agers are so in touch with their feelings—or so capable of expressing their emotional needs. It is also true that not all parents are capable of accepting their children's need for separateness without feeling personally rejected.

When bonding and separation are successfully experienced, a child is better equipped to achieve wholeness, to take responsibility for his or her own decisions, and to invent a future that is personally satisfying. Most parents want those conditions for their children—and for themselves. It is most likely to happen in families that have successfully bonded with their children very early in their relationship but who are also able to see them as separate individuals with their own agendas for their lives.

PREPARATION FOR BONDING

For many couples, preparation for bonding with their child begins even before conception. It begins when they talk about wanting a baby, when they fantasize about that child, and wonder about what kind of parents they will be. During pregnancy, most women are unconsciously using imagery to intensify their closeness with the baby and to establish the mental environment that will provide the most nurturing attitude for the infant. Some fathers are able to do this too, although, at the risk of sounding sexist, I believe the woman's preoccupation with the unborn child is far more intense. For biological reasons, she is never totally removed from the awareness of that new being developing within her.

MOTHERS AND BONDING

Elizabeth Carlin, Ph.D., a psychologist who specializes in early childhood development, stresses the importance of the parents' awareness of bonding and separation. Knowing when—and how—to encourage intimacy and then independence enables parents to gain some perspective on the nature of the relationship they are establishing with their children.

Elizabeth Carlin is a warm, intensely caring individual whose passion for her work is evident when she talks about the needs of very young children and their mothers. "It's as though the child has a right to your body those first few weeks of life to use in any way the child needs—to nurse from, to lie on, and you begin slowly to change that. For about three weeks you need to be totally immersed in the child and then, as you observe changes in the child (signs that the child's body and your body are no longer quite one) you begin to pull back. First you've adapted completely to the child's life and slowly you help the child adapt to life as you lead it, and that's separation. And that's very hard to do. Ideally, changes in the child coincide with the mother's feeling of needing to pull back, to take her ego and her body back. But mothers feel very guilty about doing that."

Working mothers often have a difficult time with feelings of guilt about separating from young children. The more they long to return to work, the more guilt they are likely to feel for leaving. When there are reality reasons, such as financial need, they experience much less guilt for doing so.

Elizabeth spoke about her own experience: When she was two years old, her mother left her to return to work. It was during the early 30's and although the obvious motivation was for financial reasons, her mother's great desire to leave the home and return to her career caused terrible guilt in the mother, which was, of course, nonverbally transmitted to the child. "I felt terribly lost, terribly deprived," she said.

One might speculate that if Elizabeth's mother had felt less guilty about the separation, the child would have felt less abandoned. If her caretakers had provided adequately for her, and her mother had communicated positive feelings about the separation, Elizabeth's response might well have been less traumatic.

A CHILD'S USE OF IMAGERY: HOW IT HELPS AND HOW IT HURTS

When children play, they are often using a form of imagery. They imagine the conversations they have with their dolls, they invent scenarios involving their stuffed animals or tractors or trains. And when their mothers leave for work, they often are able to imagine their mother's presence.

Elizabeth referred to a little girl, three or four years old, whose mother had left the child in the care of others for a very long time and yet the child managed well. "When this was discussed with the child it turned out that she would go to the mother's closet (which contained the smell of the mother, the scent of the mother's presence in the clothes and in her own personal possessions) and this provided the child with the sense of her mother's presence and with the sense that she could go on."

The child in that situation was able to use imagery to avoid a painful experience and to provide herself with what she needed. Her fantasies became positive coping skills as she kept her mother with her through the powers of her imagination. "I was not able to do that," Elizabeth said. "It wasn't that my imagery was missing; it was too filled with anger and sadness to help me cope in a better way. Children have different capacities, and kids do make choices. They make these unconscious choices at a very early age."

It isn't difficult to imagine the scenario a child might develop when she feels abandoned by a mother who is nonverbally communicating her guilt (and her desire) for leaving.

What is it that enables one child to use imagery in a positive way and what causes another child to create fantasies of abandonment and rejection and to feel overwhelming rage, sadness, and loneliness? That is a question for which there is no present answer, just as there is no current answer for why some children are survivors of atrocities and yet they function well, while others cannot function effectively in spite of loving parents and an abundance of advantages. There are mysterious ingredients involved that no one can yet explain. But if we acknowledge that at either end of the continuum these mysteries prevail, we can focus on the vast number of people who exist between these extremes.

There could be many factors in why Elizabeth created painful imagery while the imagery of the other child was positive. It could have to do with the quality of mothering that existed prior to the separation or the quality of care provided for the children by others while the mothers were gone. But Elizabeth draws upon a story told to her about the Holocaust to make her point:

> A man who survived the concentration camps was asked how he was able to endure, and he said that for each new indignity that he was asked to perform, a voice inside of him said, 'You can do it, you can do it.' And that carried him through. The importance of his statement is in the pronoun 'you'; he didn't say 'I can do it.'

It was the introjected mother saying 'You can do it.' So the people who are able to image—who are able to survive, are the people who in some way have that voice inside of them. It may be that they had the kind of mother who made that possible or it may be that these people *developed* the power to introject the mother. But somewhere they must have had something at the beginning of their lives to even start the process.

Effective bonding with our children makes it easier for them to develop the strong inner voice (the introjected mother) that can carry them through adversity all their lives. What it gives to parents when they are able to achieve this exquisite intimacy is described by Elizabeth: "I wouldn't trade the years I spent with my children for anything. Of all the things I've done in my life, bar none, it's the most important thing. It's the sum and substance in life. That doesn't mean I sat home twenty-four hours a day loving it and delighting in it. Many times I was irritable; I was impatient; I needed to get out. It was difficult but it was marvelous. I can't think of it now without feeling joy as well as tears in my eyes."

FATHERS AND BONDING

Elizabeth's husband, Maury Carlin, Ph.D, is also a child psychologist. He's an easy man to like—empathetic and confident. I asked him about fathers—about their role with their newborns and how most of them experience the bonding process:

Fathers' responses really vary; it's such an individual matter. Because I've heard of fathers—both in and out of therapy—who hardly have anything to do with the child. They don't bottle-feed the baby, or change diapers, or cuddle, or bathe the child. They don't yet see the baby as a person. I've heard that a number of times from fathers but I've never heard that from a mother. When the child is a walking, talking or semi-talking human being, then the fathers can relate. On the other side of the coin you have fathers who get up at night with the baby, even take days off from work and are really involved—but that's not typical either. Most fathers are busy out of the home; they are active human beings who delegate much of the caretaking to the mother. They return from work and, if they are psychologically minded at all, they take over with the child while the mother is preparing dinner and help with the child until the child goes to bed. That's not the ideal, but it is the way it is, a lot of the time.

The ideal would be mutually shared parenting. The father would be considerate of the mother's feelings and sometimes get up with the baby in the night; he would help with the caretaking and be sensitive to his own feelings so that he will be able to do the kind of parenting he wants to do. He would be a good soother.

One might wonder if fathers who have gone through the Lamaze classes and have been actively involved with the pregnancy are more able to experience early bonding with the child—or perhaps that is only a sign of their *wish* to be involved, and an indication of their desire to be effective parents.

It is more difficult to determine how men respond in these changing times. Many men are participating more with their young children than was the norm for a generation ago, but it is a fact that full paternal involvement is not the situation in most homes.

There are cases where the mother has been unable to bond successfully and the father has stepped in to fill this role. Maury told me about a mother who suffered a psychological trauma shortly after giving birth and the father not only bonded effectively with the child, but provided "mothering" for his wife who was in need of his attention and support.

WHEN THE BOND ISN'T FORMED

Infants who fail to bond within those early weeks of life frequently have difficulty establishing deep relationships with others, even as adults. (Remember the extremes of the continuum—there are always exceptions to any statement about human development.) There have been many psychological studies of babies raised in institutions which showed that a child who did not adequately bond was prone to physical illness, was more lethargic than the average, and later tested significantly lower than the norm in intelligence scores. Effective bonding is the foundation upon which the psychological structure of a child's life is built.

BONDING VERSUS SEPARATION

Bonding is critical to a child's happiness, but separation is just as important, if the child is to function as a healthy, independent individual. What about those cases in which a child is so close to the parents that appropriate separation is impossible? Maury told me about Allen, who is a perfect example of a child whose bonding with his parents was so intense that when he was seven years old they sought professional help—for the child's sake and for their own, as well. (The child's identity has been disguised to avoid an invasion of the family's privacy.)

> Allen is the younger child of a two child family. He is a sweet child with a mild physical disability. His brother is about three or four years older and this older boy was more powerful in terms of personality and more capable in terms of physical and emotional and intellectual prowess. Both parents were very warm and concerned, but misguided—really misguided—in their ability to effect normal separation and allow the child his individuation and personality.

Maury spoke about the child's normal nightime fears when he was four, five, even six, and those fears became reinforced by the way he could control his parents. "The boy simply would not let his parents go to sleep at night. He would insist that they stay in the room next to his bedroom and then at age five and six he was actually sleeping with them in their bed. This reinforced his fears of boogie men and robbers and terrible things happening. The parents actually believed that they were acting appropriately when they gave in to his demands. They thought this was effective parenting. But as the years progressed and he became seven years old and this behavior continued (and of course their sexual activity was severely handicapped and programmed because of his behavior) they became so irritated with him that this brought them into therapy.

> The child was not having enough emotional breathing room to develop his own individuality—to realize that nothing terrible would happen if he cried and that there was no boogie man and no disasters would occur. It was not in his emotional interests for

this kind of intense close connection they were promoting. But they were very accepting parents and when they realized that it was not in his best interest to sleep in their bed, they followed my prescription for change very well and the child was able to separate and individuate and go to sleep. There was one catch: He got a dog. The dog seemed to act as the transitional object (the substitution for the parents) and that allowed Allen to get the comfort and security that he had been getting from his parents. The dog slept in his bed and he no longer needed to sleep with his parents.

Parents often tolerate behavior that is harmful for a child because they think they are doing the "right" thing. Sometimes just recognizing the behavior as psychologically inappropriate enables them to change the way they treat the child. Everyone makes mistakes raising their children. We fail in the very areas in which we want so desperately to excel. But, for most of us, these are honest mistakes and perhaps children sense in our efforts the extent of our love and forgive us in spite of our shortcomings. If, in this Working Dream, we can gain perspective on our attitudes toward bonding and separation, we can adjust our actions and help our children through these important processes. We can hold them when they need to be held, and we can also encourage them toward independence. As Maury said, "If we do our job as parents effectively, we put ourselves right out of business."

One of the most rewarding experiences of a parent's life is when we realize that effective separation has been made and our children function effectively on their own—and enjoy coming back to us as friends.

The Working Dream will give you an opportunity to discover your feelings toward your child's independence and gain insight into how your attitude sets the stage for his or her development.

THE TRANSITION

Remember: You need your Working Dream notebook . . . a pen . . . a quiet place. Remember the series of events that will carry you into Transition as you close your eyes and experience again: a quiet beach . . . ocean sounds . . . the colors . . . the deep relaxation

. . . your personal train . . . invisible tracks moving through space and through time. (Experience the feelings through memory or by reading again pages 19–24.)

THE WORKING DREAM

Bonding and Separation (From the Parent's Point of View)

As you step from your train onto the platform of the small station you realize that you have come to this place to discover something extremely important about your relationship with your child. To gain this insight, you will need to have your child with you—so let your imagination bring your child into your Dream.

> In this Dream, whatever feelings are revealed, whatever actions are taken, no harm will come to you or your child and a valuable lesson will be learned.

In this Dream, your child will have the experience of going somewhere on a boat—so the age and maturity of your child will determine the size of the boat and the size of the body of water.

> Walk with your child down the path to the edge of the water and discover the boat that has been provided.

(If the boat and the water seem too large or too small for your child, adjust the image to the size that seems right to you.)

> If your child is an infant, the boat may be as small as an inflatable swan a baby could ride on—and the body of water may be no larger than a wading pond. If your child is a teen-ager, the boat might be a sailboat or a motorboat of substantial size. Take time to be comfortable with the boat and the water.

Notice that there is a rope keeping the boat tied to shore. What do you (or your child) do with the rope?

How long will this adventure last? An hour? All day? Even longer?

Be aware of the weather.

What provisions are on the boat?

How do you feel about your child having this experience?

How does your child seem to feel?

What do you say to each other when it is time for your child to enter the boat?

Now what happens?

Let the Dream unfold in its own way. Take your time.

What is happening now?

And what is happening now?

When the Dream is almost ended, see your child return and be aware of your feelings.

Notice how your child seems to feel.

What do you say?

What does your child say?

In the Dream, can you imagine telling your child how you feel about what you have just experienced? Can you listen to your child's experience and remain loving and support-ive, honoring the trust that is placed in you?

When it is time for the Dream to end, let your child return home first. While you are still in a dreamlike state, and before you bring yourself back to your workroom, take your Working Dream notebook and write your feelings about the events that happened in the Dream.

Now return to your workroom and when you feel alert, begin work with your Critic to comprehend the value of the Dream.

THE DREAMER AND THE CRITIC

Your reaction to your child's experience reveals many things about your relationship. Working with the metaphors that emerged in the Dream, we can begin with a few obvious assumptions: The boat and the size of the body of water are metaphors for your perception of your child's situation and capabilities at this time. Unless the child in your Dream objected to the size of the boat and asked (or demanded) that it be changed, we can assume that you assigned a boat to the child that you thought was appropriate for his or her age and maturity.

In your mind's eye, recall the size and condition of the boat. Remember you could have chosen any type of carrier, from an inflatable swan to an ocean liner. Looking as objectively as possible, do you think you chose the best boat to meet your child's needs?

It is important to remember what happened to the rope. You can see various meanings in whether the rope was coiled in preparation for returning, whether it was cut—or whether the boat was kept tethered to the shore.

If the boat remained tied to the shore by a long rope and your child is a toddler, it would certainly be advisable for you to be in the boat also. For a slightly older child, you would probably choose to swim along beside the boat. If your child is seventeen and you chose to get in the boat, swim along beside it, or keep the boat tethered, then you might want to consider whether you've been overprotective. Perhaps you want to examine the *reason* the rope exists. What makes the rope necessary? Does it exist for your needs or for your child's? What are you afraid will happen if the rope is not there?

Write in your Working Dream notebook and consider what meaning the rope plays in your perception of your child as a separate and independent person.

The following questions may help you clarify your thoughts:

Who decided how long the child would be gone? Was the decision made because of the child's needs or because of your own?

What kind of weather did you provide for your child's experience?

Was a life preserver on board? If so, did you put it there or did the child? In other words, does your child take the responsibility to prepare for possible emergencies or are you always the one who does that?

If there was food and water, who provided it?

How did each of you feel when the boat left the shore?

What kind of adventures did your child have? Was the trip uneventful and safe all the way? Were there rapids to contend with? Did other people come into the scene? What do the events and the child's response to the events tell you about your perception of your child's capabilities?

What were you doing when the child was gone? Were you watching from the shore? Having a picnic on a hill? Were you excited about the wonderful trip your child was experiencing or were you worried all the while?

Did you change in any way while the child was gone? Did your child change?

Has anything in the Dream made you aware of something that needs to change in your perception of your child? Remember, the Dream is not intended to reveal feelings or "mistakes" so that you feel guilty, but rather to reinforce your strengths or to point out areas where you can choose to parent with greater awareness and wisdom.

Variations on a Theme

In our Dreams, we are, in some significant way, all the characters that appear. Even in this last exercise, you were projecting a great deal of your own feelings onto the child in the boat. You might find it interesting, however, to imagine that you are the child and that you are in that boat. You could uncover some helpful insights about how you would react to the rope and the weather and the experiences on the water. Then you could compare your own reactions to the reactions you assigned to your child. (The script for this variation is included later in this chapter.)

Another variation on the theme would be to invite your "real" son or daughter to participate in this exercise. A child as young as four or five could enjoy "playing" with the Working Dream, although the symbols and metaphors would obviously not be meaningful. If your child is twelve or thirteen or older and willing to explore the subject of independence with you, this Inner Vision exercise can help you understand each other's feelings. Consider whether it is advisable to invite your child to experience the train and the boat-dream (using the teen-ager's script which is provided in the following exercise.)

It is extremely important to remember that when people experience a Dream they are often quite vulnerable during and after the experience. You must be especially sensitive to your child's feelings if you work together on the meaning of this Dream. All feelings need to be received without criticism. If you are loving and accepting of your differences, this Working Dream can be an effective technique for deepening communication between you.

It is also important that *you must not lead your child through the Dream.* This could be an intrusion into the unconscious material that each individual must deal with in a safe and private situation. But if your teen-ager willingly reveals to you the details about the Dream, that can be helpful to you both. It is important to remember that a child's privacy should not be violated by a parent's manipulations. Perhaps your best position is to share this chapter with your child and see if he or she is interested in experiencing the Dream to discover new awarenesses. Welcome any information that is given, but never push. And above all, never misuse any information that is given to you in trust. If this Dream is to help you resolve issues of bonding and separation, you must each realize your own responsibility to honor the feelings of the other.

If you want to experience the Dream in a way that may help you remember your own childhood feelings, imagine that you are an adolescent, walking down the path with your mother or father (or both). See if you can recall your own frustrations—which may or may not be similar to your child's responses.

If your teen-ager would like to experience the Dream and perhaps report the experience to you, the following script will be helpful. But if your teen-ager completes the experience and does not want to reveal what happened during the Dream, that need for privacy must be respected.

If you are not working with your child on this Dream, you can skip to page 178, and continue reading *Personal Stories.*

THE TRANSITION

If you are doing this Inner Vision exercise at your parent's suggestion and have not read the book, be sure to read pages 18–24 in Chapter 2 to prepare yourself for the experience. When you have completed the Transition, you are ready to begin the Working Dream.

THE WORKING DREAM

Bonding and Separation (From a Teen-ager's Point of View)

As you step from your train onto the platform of the small station you realize that you have come to this place to discover something extremely important about your relationship with your parents. To gain this insight, you will need to have them with you in fantasy, so let your imagination bring your parents into the Dream.

In this Dream, whatever feelings are revealed, whatever actions are taken, no harm will come to you or your parents and a valuable lesson will be learned.

In this Dream, you will have the experience of going somewhere on a boat and you will determine the size of the boat and the size of the body of water.

Walk with your parents down the path to the edge of the water and discover the boat that has been provided for you.

(If the boat and the water seem too large or too small for you, adjust the image to the size that seems right to you.)

Take time to be comfortable with the boat and the water.

Notice that there is a rope keeping the boat tied to shore. What do you (or your parents) do with the rope?

How long will this adventure last? An hour? All day? Even longer?

Be aware of the weather.

What provisions are in the boat?

How do you feel as you anticipate your experience on the boat?

How do your parents seem to feel?

What do you say to each other when it is time for you to leave?

As the boat pulls away from the shore, your own imagination will determine what happens. No harm will come to you but you will have an interesting experience on the boat or on the shores of a distant land or anyplace that you choose to travel in your boat.

Let the Dream unfold in its own way. Take your time.

What is happening now?

And what is happening now?

When the Dream is almost ended, you are coming back to the place of your departure. You can see your parents. What are you feeling now?

Notice how your parents seem to feel.

What do you say to them?

What do they say to you?

Now imagine telling your parents what you felt and what you experienced on your trip. Are they able to listen to you and honor your feelings? Can you imagine listening while they reveal their feelings? Can you listen to them and honor their feelings, as well?

When it is time for the Dream to end, let your parents return home first. While you are still in a dreamlike state, and before you bring yourself back to your workroom, take your notebook and write your feelings about the events that happened in the Dream.

Now return to your workroom and when you are alert, begin work with your Critic to comprehend the value of the Dream.

THE DREAMER AND THE CRITIC

Your reaction to the experiences you had during the Dream reveals many things about your relationship with your parents. Working with the metaphors that emerged in the Dream, we can begin with a few obvious assumptions: The boat and the size of the body of water are metaphors for your perception of your situation and capabilities at this time in your life.

In your mind's eye, recall the size and condition of the boat. Remember you could have chosen any type of carrier, from a rowboat to an ocean liner. Does the size, type, and condition of the boat reveal anything about the way you feel about yourself?

Your perception of the rope that tied the boat to shore will help you understand your feelings about your independence. What happened to the rope and who made the decision about it?

Does the rope exist because of your needs or because of your parents'? What would happen if the rope wasn't there?

Who decided how long you would be gone? Did you make the decision or did your parents make it for you?

Consider the kind of weather you provided for your trip. Was a life preserver on board? If so, did you put it there or did your parents?

If there was food and water, who provided it?

What kind of adventures did you have during the Dream?

What were your parents doing while you were gone? Did they change in any way? Did you change?

Has anything in the Dream made you aware of something that needs to change in your perception of yourself or your parents?

If you are experiencing this Inner Vision exercise in partnership with your parents, you can use the metaphors in this Dream to help them understand your feelings—and to help you understand theirs.

Personal Stories

When Sandra and her sixteen-year-old daughter, Lauren, each experienced the Working Dream, the relationship between them hadn't been close for some time. Still, they were both willing to work together in the Inner Vision process and that indicated a flexibility of attitude on both their parts.

The season of Sandra's Dream was placed in winter and the gray afternoon sky turned dark along the horizon, as if a storm was brewing far in the distance. She felt anxious and watched in silence as Lauren jerked the rope free; there was so much Sandra wanted to say, but in the Dream no words would form and a terrible sense of loss engulfed her. Sandra imagined that her daughter's motorboat had an engine so powerful that the force of it overwhelmed the frail wooden hull. While Lauren was gone, Sandra sat by the side of the lake and worried: She didn't know if food or water was on board (she had thought of it earlier but had felt ambivalent about providing it—as if that was something Lauren should do for herself). Sandra had seen life preservers on board but didn't know if they were the right kind. Images came in quick sequence—the motor racing out of control . . . another boat full of kids heading toward Lauren . . . the darkening sky. The Dream shifted and there were flashbacks to Sandra's own youth. She remembered being in a car, driving home alone from a friend's house through a dark stretch of country road . . . another car close behind her, swerving, honking, flashing lights. The past took over and held her—she pulled herself free and fled from the memories into the present. Sandra thought of Lauren and brought her back into the Dream, watching her return from the boat ride. She wanted to rush toward Lauren and hold her close but was only able to say "I'm glad you're home."

In Sandra's associations to the Dream, she realized that the powerful motor and frail boat was an accurate image for the way she perceived her daughter; she thought of Lauren as a young woman driven by powerful forces of emotion that were strong and potentially destructive. Sandra was afraid when Lauren went out alone, but she also worried about her daughter's friends, who seemed wild and irresponsible. Sandra thought of her own youth and a dangerous situation that had been frightening (although nothing terrible had happened). The Dream had seemed terrifying and it was with great relief that Sandra brought it to a close.

Lauren, on the other hand, had a terrific Dream. Her imagination created a sailboat on a peaceful lake. It was a warm summer day and she left without any significant remarks to her mother. She had prepared a picnic lunch, checked the boat for supplies, turned on the music she liked, and set out across the lake where she stopped on a beautiful island and was joined by her boyfriend. The fantasies she reported were romantic and very tender, indicative of a young woman who has some high expectations for what a caring relationship should be. Reluctantly she ended the Dream and returned home.

Comparing notes brought few surprises for Lauren; she was all to familiar with her mother's anxieties and doubts about her activities. But she was touched by the story her mother told her—of being curbed by a carload of boys and "rescued" by the unlikely appearance of a passing motorist who chose to get involved. And for the first time, Lauren said she could understand the reality of her mother's fears when she was out alone at night.

Communication was more open between them than it had been for some time. They agreed that there needed to be more laughter in the home, less constant concern about Lauren's activities. It was a time for separation—a time of preparation for the following year, when Lauren would leave for college. Lauren needed to pull away from the intensity of her mother's attention—but Sandra needed more assurances that Lauren was being responsible about important choices.

They were both amused by the difference in their images of the boat—Lauren could see how her mother might choose a boat with a motor too powerful for her size, for her anger was quick and verbal and she often cried during her outbursts of temper. (Other powerful emotions that might have concerned Sandra were not mentioned.)

Sandra's reluctance to supply the food and water indicated her desire to let Lauren take care of herself in the "transition year." Lauren pointed out that she had been doing a pretty good job of that for some time and Sandra agreed that was true.

Lauren volunteered that she wasn't always thoughtful about letting her mother know where she was—and with whom—and she confessed to doing this pruposefully because she resented all of the careful controlling of her life. When she imagined her mother's feelings during the boat ride, she offered to be more considerate in the future.

The Dream provided a safe and inviting situation where Lauren could express her need for more independence and Sandra could talk about her fears of separation. They were both able to deal with a volatile subject with compassion for the other's feelings—and finally, to express their love for each other, which neither of them had been able to do for a very long time.

Building Blocks

Whether you use this Dream with your child or privately, the metaphors should help you perceive how you feel about the issue of bonding and separation. If you experience this Dream several times over a period of months, you may discover that you use the metaphors differently—the script changes. If you save your Working Dream notebook and make careful notes each time you experience the Dream, it can be extremely interesting to see how your perceptions change—and how your relationship with your child changes, as a result of your new insights.

CHAPTER 14

IMAGING FOR PEACE

◆

Someday after we have mastered the air, the winds, the tides, and gravity, we will harness for God the energies of love. And then, for the second time in the history of the world man will have discovered fire.

Pierre Teilhard de Chardin took a long look into the future and saw that it was good. When is the last time you heard someone comment about the future of the world in such positive terms? We are realists, after all; we read the papers, watch the news. Perhaps we have seen too much—our children have seen too much—to ever again believe that the world is becoming a better place. Prophets of doom are no longer holy men calling the world to repentance—they are fifth- and sixth-grade children discussing nuclear destruction as if time has run out and there is nothing anyone can do.

In *Late Night Thoughts on Listening to Mahler's Ninth Symphony*, Lewis Thomas contemplated the end of humanity by nuclear holocaust. He referred to a government pamphlet describing the destructive power of the MX missiles and a Sunday afternoon television program discussing the evacuation of our cities in the event that we were attacked by equally powerful missiles from the other side. "If I were very young," he wrote, "sixteen or seventeen years old, I think I would begin, perhaps very slowly and imperceptibly, to go crazy. . . . If I were sixteen or seventeen years old and had to listen to that, or read things like that, I would want to give up listening and reading. I would begin thinking up new kinds of sounds, different from any music heard before, and I would be twisting and turning to rid myself of human language."

If any civilization believes that it is doomed to bring about the destruction of humanity, how can it envision other possibilities? Think of self-fulfilling prophecies and how they condition the actions of even one person—now multiply that by the number of people on the earth—and *then* consider the power of negative perceptions and how they are operating in our society. Perhaps our greatest danger comes from within our own minds—when we can no longer believe that there is anything we can do to influence the future.

Time *is* running out—but we are not victims unless we choose to be.

Roger Sperry, winner of the Nobel Prize in 1981 for his revolutionary work on the human brain, strongly believes there are choices we could make that would correct present trends and secure the world's future. "The key lies in human value priorities, a new value system more in tune with today's reality and our changing views of brain and consciousness," he said to me one day in his office at Caltech. "The world needs a global ethic that will raise our sights above national self interest to higher, more long range values."

Roger Sperry has formulated an "ideology" that merges his humanistic science with the evolving spirituality of man. He has not given up on us yet. Now in his seventies, he talks with passion about the future and about his dream to raise the consciousness of the world's scientific, religious, and political leaders so that they will unite in a commitment to global responsibility, to protect for coming generations, the evolving quality of our biosphere.

It's all worked out," he said, "the ideas, the logic, the 'left-brain' appeal is all there—even the endorsement of science in the consciousness revolution. What we need now is the emotional and personal appeal—the right-brain contribution. To reverse present trends is going to require counter forces of the most powerful kind. People have to see that the most sacred things—the meaning of life—the higher meaning of *everything* is at stake.

His eyes softened and somewhere, mid-sentence, a smile framed the challenge: "We need new psalms for the people. You could write them." The silence that followed was not without its dramatic effect. For a scientist, that man has a great sense of theater: He knew exactly how long to let the thought play in my imagination before moving on.

For more than a year, I have thought about Roger Sperry's gentle challenge and taken it to heart. We do need new psalms for the people, but perhaps the psalms are not just words—they could be pictures in the mind's eye. Perhaps the psalms could be Working Dreams, and each Dreamer would have a place within the structure of the Dream for his or her personal vision. Imaging for peace is not a new concept. By various names and in a variety of ways, alone and in groups, in this country and in others, there are people who have imagined the best of all possibilities. Using the process of Inner Vision, a plan occurred to me that could extend the value and the impact of these images. It has the following advantages:

- It involves the Working Dream and therefore can alter the perception of the Dreamer.

- It goes beyond the Dream and requires a certain action on the part of the Dreamer.

- It has the potential to influence billions of people.

- It requires of you, as Dreamer, these two things: communication with two people soon after your experience with the Working Dream, and the commitment of three minutes a day for as long as you believe in the power of this process.

WORKING DREAMS AND WORKING REALITIES

By now, you have seen how your personal imagery works to alter your perception, and therefore to influence your actions. There is nothing magical to it. Although there are those who will tell you that our personal imagery transcends the boundaries of our minds and merges in the collective unconscious with the thoughts of others, most scientists would take a dim view of that supposition; there is no evidence to support such wishful thinking. However, many people are convinced that our collective thoughts do have the power to influence the thinking of others. If that *is* true, let our dreams support the highest possible good—but if it is *not* true, let us rely upon another way to invent the future with our Dreams.

PREPARATION FOR THE DREAM

You don't need your Working Dream notebook, or a pen or your usual workplace. In preparation for this Dream you need only the commitment of three minutes a day at a consistent time. You might choose the time just before you fall asleep, when you enter the twilight state automatically. If so, the Dream could influence you through the night at some preconscious level.

You might choose the first three minutes of the morning, when the tone of the Dream can establish your center of peace for the day. Your perceptions can be influenced by the power of love that was generated in the Dream.

You may choose a special time when you meditate or pray, when you watch the sunset or the sunrise, when you look over your appointments for the day, or rock your baby to sleep. Choose the time that is right for you but let it be a special time when you offer as your gift to the world three minutes of your concentration and your positive energy for peace.

You may want to begin by using images you learned from the Transition . . . the beach . . . the train . . . the invisible tracks. Perhaps you no longer need this specific imagery to enter the Dreamscape for you may be able to achieve the altered awareness by taking one deep breath and transporting yourself into the twilight state in that one instant. Do whatever is best for you.

THE WORKING DREAM

Imaging for Peace

Begin by transporting yourself to a place that creates in you a feeling of peace, of harmony with the universe, and gratitude for all that is good. Breathe in the feeling of peace and of appreciation.

Imagine that any resentment or hostility that has evolved in your spirit drains from your body and in its place a sense of contentment resonates throughout your being.

Love that is so unselfish and so pure that it transcends human understanding is known as *agape*. Sense the presence above you of this perfect form of love. Imagine it in the form of a golden light. Open your hands and imagine that the light touches your palms and is absorbed into your body.

> And the golden light of love moves into all parts of your body, filling you with the power of *agape*.
> The golden light is stronger than any resentment that has held you in bondage and it sets you free to experience the fullness of love.

In your mind's eye you see a baby or a young child and you imagine the golden light reaching out to the child, filling the child with love. You see a man and a woman who are very old and you wish them peace. You see lovers and you wish them joy.

> In this Dream, you have the power to transport yourself to any place in the world and to become one with the people in that land. You have the power to see them before your eyes and to hear them and to touch them and to know them as you would know a brother or a sister you had not seen for a very long time. You have the power to love those who are not pleasing you—which is a gift as valuable as emeralds and as precious as pearls.

Let your thoughts carry you across the earth to another land and you see a child who has skin that is a different color and hair that is another texture and eyes that are shaped differently than your own—but as you look into those eyes you recognize the soul of the child, which could be the soul of your own child, and you feel love. And you wish for peace.

> In that land, or another land that is also foreign to you, you see an old woman or an old man whose eyes meet yours and

you feel a kinship with the soul of that person and you feel a
sense of bonding and you wish for peace.

Your thoughts carry you to another land where you find young
lovers and are touched by their love. . . . In them you see yourself and your parents and your children and the children who are
yet to be born and you love them all and you wish them peace.

When you return to your place of departure you resolve
that this day you will live in a way that promotes peace and
you will reject choices that are detrimental to peace and
you will rise above all fear that keeps you from a spirit of
love.

By the strength of your will you choose peace. By the power of
your mind you choose love. And as you move from the Working
Dream into your daily reality, you retain all that will contribute to
peace within yourself and to peace on earth.

THE DREAMER AND THE CRITIC

If it did nothing more, this Working Dream would enable you to
live a life of greater compassion and personal contentment. But if
this Dream enables you to commit your energies to actions of love
and of peace, you will have risen above the fantasy to the reality of
the Dream.

If you tell two people about the Working Dream and teach
those two people to image and perhaps lead them through the
Dream, and if those people each promise to teach two other people and each of those to teach two more—you will have initiated a
chain reaction of love that could encircle the world.

If you do this, you will be like the wise steward in the ancient
fable who extracted a promise from the king to give him a penny
and the next day to double it and each day to double the sum of his
coins until, as of course you know, he soon became a billionaire. If
we can increase the number of people committed to global responsibility, as the steward increased the number of his coins, our

wealth will be in terms of love—our treasure will be peace on earth.

If one person told only two people and if those two kept the promise and on the next day told two more, and so on and so on as the progression continues, in twenty days more than a million people could be imaging for peace. Within thirty days more than a billion people could be involved. Within thirty-two days, the entire population of the earth could be aware that the future is ours to determine.

As realists, we know that changing the world in this way will not happen so suddenly. But between the Dream and the reality lie a multitude of possibilities. If we concentrate on the work we are to do, the numbers will take care of themselves.

This book will be read in other lands and there will be people in other countries who tell two people and each of those will tell two more, and although some will break the chain, others will start again, as new progressions of love are initiated. Many will begin making choices for peace in their personal lives and in their political attitudes; governments will feel the impact of those perceptions.

There are days when you will doubt the power of the imagery; create the images and as you do, faith will return. There are days that logic will remind you of the host of people who will never dream for peace; create the images and as you do, commitment will return. There are days you will be busy and not believe that you have three minutes in which to participate in saving the world. Create the images and as you do, know that there are others, like yourself, working for peace.

Of all the things we will strive to accomplish in our lives, nothing is more important than to harness the energies of love to make the dream of peace a reality—if not for God's sake or for our own, then for the children.

KEEPING IN TOUCH

Your responses to Inner Vision techniques are of great interest to me and if you would like to share your experiences or participate in future research projects, I would be pleased to hear from you.

Marilee Zdenek
Right-Brain Resources, Inc.
Reseda Medical Building
7012 Reseda Blvd., Suite SW 101
Reseda, CA   91335

TAPES AND SEMINARS

Information regarding seminars and audiocassette tapes for the imagery exercises in *Inventing the Future* and *The Right-Brain Experience* may be obtained by writing to Right-Brain Resources, Inc. (Att: Educational Services), at the above address or by calling (818) 883-1232.

SOURCES FOR QUOTATIONS

Buscaglia, Leo. *Loving Each Other.* New Jersey: Slack, Incorporated, 1984.

Champlin, Charles. Review of *The Ultimate Seduction* by Charlotte Chandler. *Los Angeles Times*, May 19, 1984, Section 5, page 1.

Chandler, Charlotte. *The Ultimate Seduction.* New York: Doubleday and Company, 1984.

Eiseley, Loren. *Notes of an Alchemist.* New York: Charles Scribner's Sons, 1972.

Ellis, Havelock. *The Dance of Life.* copyright 1923 by Havelock Ellis.

Fisher, Roger. *Getting to Yes.* New York: Penguin Books, 1981.

Frankle, Victor E., M.D. *The Doctor and the Soul.* New York: Alfred A. Knopf, 1965.

Harvey, Steve. "Running on Courage Every Step of the Way." *Los Angeles Times*, February 19, 1985, Section 2, page 1.

Huxley, Aldous. epigraph in *The Choice Is Always Ours* edited by Dorothy Berkley Phillips; co-edited by Elizabeth Boyden Howes and Lucille M. Nixon. New York and Evanston: Harper and Row, 1948.

Rilke, Rainer Maria. *Letters to a Young Poet.* New York: W.W. Norton and Company, 1963.

Rostand, Jean. *The Substance of Man.* Westport, Connecticut: Greenwood, 1973.

Teilhard de Chardin, Pierre. *The Phenomenon of Man.* New York: Harper and Row, 1955.

Thomas, Lewis. *Late Night Thoughts on Listening to Mahler's Ninth Symphony.* New York: The Viking Press, 1980–1983.

Thoreau, Henry David. *Walden and Civil Disobedience.* New York/London: W.W. Norton and Company, 1966.

Zdenek, Marilee and Champion, Marge. *God Is a Verb!* Waco, Texas: Word Books, 1974.

Zukav, Gary. *The Dancing Wu Li Masters.* New York: Bantam Books, 1972.

INDEX

◆

ABOUT THE AUTHOR

Marilee Zdenek is the author of six books including the best seller, *The Right-Brain Experience*. She has written for the theater and reviews books for "The Los Angeles Times." She is also founder and president of Right-Brain Resources, Inc., a consulting firm that provides seminars and tapes that stimulate creative thinking. Lecturing in Europe and the United States, she has spoken before audiences of engineers, writers, entrepreneurs, corporate executives, doctors, psychologist, and educators. On several occasions she has addressed political and economic world leaders for the EMF's (European Management Foundation's) Davos Symposium in Switzerland.

Her interest in creative thought processes and their link to discoveries in brain research originated while she was working in various milieux as lyricist, poet, actress, and liturgist. This fascination with how imagery and specific right-brain activities could enhance the powers of imagination led her to twelve years of research working with psychobiologists, psychiatrists, and neurologists. During this time, she created two unique programs, "The Right-Brain Experience" and "Inner Vision." These techniques induce creative thought processes and can be applied to many facets of personal and professional development.

Marilee Zdenek has served on the Board of Directors of three hospitals and, for two years, was Executive Vice-President of PEN, Los Angeles Center. She lives in Los Angeles with her husband, Albert N. Zdenek, M.D., and has two daughters, Gina and Tamara.